1855

EDITOR'S NOTE

This book includes only those châteaux listed in the 1855 Classification of Bordeaux Wines, members of the Conseil des Grands Crus Classés en 1855 (Médoc & Sauternes), under the direction of Sylvain Boivert, director.

MÉDOC & SAUTERNES

BORDEAUX 1855

A GUIDE TO THE
GRANDS CRUS CLASSÉS

Foreword by
Stéphane Bern

Flammarion

↑
Gruaud Larose
(Saint-Julien appellation)

THIS UNIQUE GUIDE, PUBLISHED BY FLAMMARION, INVITES US TO BORDEAUX TO DISCOVER THE GRANDS CRUS CLASSÉS OF 1855 THROUGH THE REGION'S EXCEPTIONAL HERITAGE AND REMARKABLE LANDSCAPES.

PHILIPPE CASTÉJA
PRESIDENT,
CONSEIL DES GRANDS CRUS CLASSÉS
EN 1855 (MÉDOC & SAUTERNES)

CONTENTS

BORDEAUX
GRANDS CRUS CLASSÉS 1855

ESSENTIAL INFORMATION

FOREWORD

AN INCREDIBLE HERITAGE

BY STÉPHANE BERN

Historical, as well as architectural, natural, gastronomic, and intangible: the heritage of Bordeaux's grands crus classés has been synonymous with French excellence for nearly one hundred and sixty years. This epic story began in 1855 at the World's Fair, organized in Paris by Emperor Napoleon III. The owners of Bordeaux's vineyards were asked to present the best of French terroir—that is, the most popular and sought-after grand crus, which were divided into five categories. Since then, the eighty-seven estates featured in the classification have helped shape the international reputations of Médoc and Sauternes, working tirelessly to perfect the charming wines produced in the appellations of Margaux, Saint-Julien, Pauillac, or Saint-Estèphe, among others. This is, indeed, a remarkable heritage, for although Bordeaux's châteaux are of great architectural and historical interest, they are also recognized around the world thanks to their

Stéphane Bern

labels, which travel to every corner of the globe, offering the promise of reverie, pleasure, and incredible flavors, all contained in a bottle. Rather than evoking military feats, sieges, or battles, their names reflect the relentless work of those who cultivate the richness of the terroir and strive to develop a distinctly French art de vivre, with all of its sophisticated expertise: Château Lafite-Rothschild, Château Latour, Château Margaux, Château Mouton-Rothschild, Château Haut-Brion, and, of course, Château d'Yquem, to cite only the premiers crus in Médoc and the premier cru supérieur in Sauternes. But there are many other charming estates to visit and savor on this list. These châteaux form a map of French heritage sites, even if some visitors are more interested in viewing casks and cellars than ballrooms or fortifications. Those in search of this patrimony will be captivated by the verdant backdrop that sets off the estates—not formal gardens, but vineyards stretching as far as the eye can see. The 1855 grands crus classés form an exceptional ensemble united by a common destiny that nevertheless allows for an abundant diversity of varietals as well as architectural constructions. Does any other region in France enjoy such worldwide renown? Each bottle, each label, extends an invitation to travel, to embark on a voyage to Bordeaux, on the banks of the majestic Garonne River, from the port that enabled international trade to flourish and where the Cité du Vin now stands. This unique inheritance, made up of a multitude of châteaux and winemaking estates surrounding a city of art and history, is a tremendous touristic asset for France. Cultivating its terroir and its traditions with brio, this entire region now offers visitors an immersive experience in a marvelous world where the beauty of the sites, the power of history, and the ingenuity of winemakers come together with the delicacy of the wines. This fruitful marriage has given rise to a thriving wine tourism industry, and this book invites you to discover the châteaux, museums, cellars, restaurants, and tasting rooms that celebrate the region's priceless heritage.

THE SETTING

BORDEAUX: A WELCOMING CITY

No other city in the world is as intimately tied to the history, prestige, and culture of wine. Listed as a UNESCO World Heritage Site, Bordeaux is known the world over, and its name calls to mind a certain French *art de vivre* that is exemplified in this historic winegrowing region recognized for its excellence.

THE ORIGINS

BORDEAUX THROUGH THE CENTURIES

The history of Bordeaux is intertwined with its terroirs, which inform the region's identity and are the basis for the favorable relations it has cultivated with other areas of the world over the centuries.

From Antiquity to the Middle Ages
Biturica, an ancestor of the Cabernet grape variety, was grown along the banks of the Garonne as far back as Roman times. Burdigala, an early name for Bordeaux, was one of the most important centers of trade in the imperial province of Gallia Aquitania, which in 70 CE extended from the Pyrenees mountains to the Loire River. Emperor Vespasian declared Burdigala the province's administrative capital. The poet Ausonius, born around 309 CE in Aquitaine, mentions the vineyards of Médoc and his love of Pauillac in his letters to Theon.

After several centuries fraught with invasions by the Vandals, then the Visigoths and the Franks in the early fifth century, Bordeaux became one of the prominent cities in the Duchy of Aquitaine, established in 675 CE. Four centuries later, following the death of William X, rule of the region fell to Eleonor, who was crowned queen of France in 1137, in Bourges, after her marriage to Louis VII. Guests at their wedding would have sipped on wine from the Issan vineyards.

From the tenth to the fifteenth century
Bordeaux was surrounded by a vast mosaic of plots where vines grew on trellises at eye level. At a time when clean water was a rare commodity, wine was a staple and consumed at an average rate of 3 quarts (3 L) per day and per person (at the time, wine averaged 7 or 8 percent alcohol).

The troubled marriage between Eleonor and Louis the Pious was annulled on May 18, 1152. Eight weeks later, Eleonor married the future king of England, Henry Plantagenet, in Poitiers. Their marriage marked the beginning of several centuries of favorable relations between the province of La Guyenne and England, which would play a crucial role in the evolution of Bordeaux wines.

Eleanor introduced a new *art de vivre* at court, one far removed from the coarse manners that had defined it up to that point. The troubadours in her entourage recited poems that extolled the ideals of *fine amor* (courtly love), associated with fine food and drink—not least of all, wine.

Aquitaine came under the protection of the English Crown for three centuries, a boon for wine producers and merchants who discovered a demanding but loyal market, and one that was far more reliable than the neighboring duchies, which required purchasers to travel roads that were often unsafe. Bordeaux could be reached directly via the Gironde estuary, giving the city a significant advantage over competing winemaking regions like Burgundy and Champagne.

This trade brought great prosperity to Bordeaux and endeared its population to the English. Favorable relations continued until the end of the Hundred Years' War, which was, in fact, decided in Bordeaux. The city was besieged by Charles VII's armies until the Battle of Castillon erupted in July 1453. This confrontation marked England's defeat, illustrated with verve by the death of a legendary general, John Talbot, who was nicknamed the "Terror of the French" and whose memory is honored to this day by a grand cru classé in Saint-Julien: Château Talbot. The name Château Batailley also celebrates a crucial moment in French history: after being captured, Bordeaux was invaded by the French Crown in Gascony, with disastrous consequences for wine cultivation and trade, which were wiped out by a punishing tax.

A reputation is born

Bordeaux underwent something of a renaissance in the seventeenth century. Dutch engineers began draining the marshes in Médoc, and their compatriots began importing the region's wines, particularly sweet, dry white wines intended for distillation.

At the same time, the Pontac family of Château Haut-Brion began developing New French Claret and made every

"Bordeaux, a city lovingly designed, a city perfect for walking and wonder, and the gateway to time! In Bordeaux, we can set out without a destination, sure to find ourselves standing before a marvel." —FRANÇOIS MAURIAC

Château Haut-Brion
Premier cru classé, Pessac

effort to win over the British clientele; following the Great Fire of 1666, they opened a fashionable eating house in London: Pontac's Head. There, England's high society and intelligentsia discovered New French Claret, the first red wine to approximate today's wines. Auguste Pontac developed various techniques, such as topping up and racking, which enabled him to improve wine preservation and led to the accidental discovery of its beneficial effect on taste. Long before it became a grand cru classé in the 1855 classification, Château Haut-Brion would be the first *grand vin* named after its producer and its terroir.

Bordeaux first appeared at the court of Versailles in the mid-eighteenth century. The Duke of Richelieu, great-nephew of the famous cardinal and governor of Guyenne, convinced Louis XV to abandon wine from Burgundy and Champagne in favor of wine from Bordeaux, praising its medicinal benefits.

During the French Revolution, members of the Gironde political faction mounted a resistance to the radical Montagnards, an opposing political group, for which the residents of Bordeaux and the owners of neighboring châteaux were made to pay dearly.

The nineteenth century was plagued with epidemics and outbreaks of downy mildew in the early 1850s, followed by the ravages of phylloxera, which appeared in Bordeaux in 1866, and powdery mildew. In 1886, at Château Dauzac, botanist Alexis Millardet developed a fungicide to fight mildews—inspired by a treatment common in Médoc called *bouille bordelaise,* or "Bordeaux mixture"—using copper sulfate and lime. Paradoxically, this was also a golden age for French winemaking thanks to technological advances and the emergence of markets in Germany, Belgium, the Netherlands, Switzerland, and Russia, which led to a new diversity in wine styles.

The region was poised to assert its reputation on the world stage and introduce the prestigious châteaux of the 1855 classification to a growing number of countries.

A FRANCO-AMERICAN FRIENDSHIP

A SPECIAL RELATIONSHIP WITH THE UNITED STATES

On Place Picard, a few minutes' walk from Place des Quinconces, a replica of the Statue of Liberty is a discreet reminder of the important role that Bordeaux has played in the longstanding friendship between France and the United States.

Lafayette

On the eve of the French Revolution, the Marquis de Lafayette set sail from the port of Pauillac carrying food, arms, and ammunition to assist the American separatists, despite outright opposition from his family and King Louis XVI, who feared that his action would trigger a new war with England.

A previous expedition leaving from Le Havre and organized by Beaumarchais had been cut short by royal forces. So Lafayette decided to distance himself from Paris and make use of the Gironde's independence to keep his departure a secret. He discreetly financed the purchase of a commercial ship constructed in a shipyard in Bacalan, which he renamed *La Victoire*. He set sail in April 1777, headed for Charleston, South Carolina. Once he arrived, he gradually earned George Washington's trust and became the future president's aide-de-camp and one of his most valuable allies.

Three wine-loving American presidents

The first three American presidents were particularly fond of wine, and while George Washington favored Madeira (he tried, unsuccessfully, to cultivate the grape at Mount Vernon), John Adams and Thomas Jefferson appear to have shared a taste for the great wines of Médoc.

In 1778, Adams requested a list of four premiers crus ("Chateau Margeaux, Hautbrion, La Fitte, and Latour"), while Jefferson traveled to Bordeaux in May 1787. He began his stay with a visit to Château d'Yquem, then traveled to other estates, including Château Haut-Brion; he had been served the château's wine for the first time at the table of Benjamin Franklin. He ordered twenty-four cases of Haut-Brion, two hundred and fifty bottles of Château Lafite, and an unknown quantity of Château d'Yquem.

Jefferson established a classification divided into three categories of grand crus; several of these châteaux would later be included in the 1855 Classification. His first category crus were Château Margaux, La Tour de Segur (Château Latour), Hautbrion (Château Haut-Brion), and Château de

La Fite (Château Lafite-Rothschild). Then, in his second category, he mentions Rozan (Château Rauzan-Ségla), Dabbadie (Château Beychevelle), Lionville (Château Léoville), La Rose (Château Gruaud-Larose), Quirouen (Château Kirwan), and Durfort (Château Durfort-Viviens). And lastly, his list cites "Calons" (Château Calons-Segur), "Mouton" (Château Mouton-Rothschild), "Gassie" (Château Rauzan-Gassies), "Arboete" (Château Lagrange), "Pontette" (Château Pontet-Canet), "de Terme" (Château Marquis de Terme), and "Candale" (Château d'Issan).

"The French are so proud of their wines that they have given some of their cities the name of a grand cru." —OSCAR WILDE

THE *HERMIONE*

This frigate is a replica of the vessel that transported the Marquis de Lafayette on his third trip to the United States. When it was launched in October 2014, it docked at Quai Richelieu in Bordeaux. To help finance this outstanding project, writer Erik Orsenna, member of the Académie Française and president of the Hermione-Lafayette Foundation, announced that the complete collection of 2010 vintages from the 1855 Classification (eighty-seven bottles) would be donated by the Conseil des Grands Crus Classés of 1855. The collection was sold to an American couple, Bob and Marilyn Fisher, who were touched by the *Hermione* project and by its educational mission to foster relations between France and the United States. Following in the footsteps of Thomas Jefferson, they spent several days in 2015 visiting a selection of 1855 grands crus classés.

HÔTEL FENWICK

Bordeaux hosted the first United States diplomatic representative when the Continental Congress sent John Bondfield there in March 1778, several weeks after France formally recognized the thirteen colonies as an independent nation. In 1790, Hôtel Fenwick was built on the Quai des Chartrons to host the first consul sent by George Washington. Today, the building is still used for diplomatic purposes—a reminder of the longstanding friendship between the two nations.

WINE COULD BE ANOTHER WORD FOR FRIENDSHIP.

—ERIK ORSENNA

←
The *Hermione*'s maiden voyage
2014

CLARET

The word "claret" is still used in English to refer to a red *grand vin* from Bordeaux—which may come as a surprise, since the beverage in question is not known for its clear or light color. In fact, the origin of the word dates back to the sixteenth century, when wine was made by blending every grape variety, was consumed young, and was somewhere between modern Bordeaux and rosé wine in color. A contemporary appellation exists for Bordeaux-Clairets, a family of wines known for their lighter qualities.

DID YOU KNOW?

The name "Guyenne," used since the thirteenth century to refer to the Plantagenet's holdings in Aquitaine, is the result of a sound change from the Latin word "*Aquitania*" to the old Gascon word "*Aguiania*," then to the modern French term "*la Guyenne*."

TANNINS: A SECRET TO GOOD HEALTH

"Is Your Majesty not aware that I have found the famous Fountain of Youth?" replied the Duke of Richelieu to King Louis XV, who had expressed his surprise at the fifty-nine-year-old's apparent vigorous health; the duke was referring to his discovery of Château Lafite. The great-nephew of the famous cardinal claimed tannins were responsible for the wine's beneficial effects on the king's intestinal complaints.

On the eve of the 1855 classification, the former wine merchant Mr. Saint-Amant, author of the outstanding work *Promenade en Médoc*, published the same year, claimed to be speaking with strict scientific objectivity when he declared that "Bordeaux wine, pure and carefully chosen, acts effectively on the stomach while respecting the brain," noting that "it keeps the breath sweet and the mouth fresh." According to this specialist, these virtues stem from tannins that, associated with ferrous salts unique to the terroir found on the banks of the Gironde estuary, make the region's wines "the best infusion for maintaining or restoring good blood health."

→
Château Prieuré-Lichine
Quatrième cru classé, Margaux

↑
Château d'Yquem
Premier cru
classé supérieur,
Sauternes

VISITS AND TASTINGS

BORDEAUX: AN ESSENTIAL DESTINATION

Bordeaux is home to many must-see sites, where you can immerse yourself in the city's history, deepen your knowledge of wine and winemaking, and taste a large selection of crus classés.

Bar à Vin

The ground floor of the Maison du Vin de Bordeaux is home to Bar à Vin: the ideal place to discover a new wine, get advice from a group of true enthusiasts, or simply enjoy a glass of wine in an exceptional setting.

Red, sweet or dry white, rosé, clairet, crémant: the diversity of Bordeaux wines is represented on the bar's menu, which is regularly updated. Permanent fixtures include some

Bar à Vin and
Hôtel Gobineau
3 Cours du 30-Juillet
33 000 Bordeaux
baravin.bordeaux.com

thirty wines that have been blind selected by the Conseil Interprofessionnel des Vins de Bordeaux and are served exclusively by the glass. If you feel like it, you can pair them with platters of local cheese, charcuterie, or chocolate.

The Maison du Vin de Bordeaux occupies an eighteenth-century building known as the Hôtel Gobineau and houses the headquarters of the Interprofessional Council of Bordeaux Wines and the Conseil des Grands Crus Classés en 1855. Entirely designed and renovated by architect Françoise Bousquet, the space calls to mind the prow of a ship with a blend of neoclassical, colonnade architecture and contemporary furniture, and uses fine materials that resonate with the world of winemaking.

Several atmospheres await patrons: a cozy area featuring low tables and armchairs; a space where tables and chairs are spread out to allow more privacy; and a bar area with high tables and a bistro feel. In summer, a sunny terrace offers a view on the Grand Théâtre.

Wine is also celebrated in the artwork adorning the interiors, including a vine-themed Aubusson tapestry and two stained-glass windows by René Buthaud depicting a triumphant Apollo surrounded by grape harvesters in Bordeaux.

Cité du Vin

Before or after immersing yourself in the singular world of the 1855 crus classés, make sure you spend a few hours, or even a whole day, at this utterly unique site that celebrates the richness and diversity of wine's cultural, universal, and living heritage through the ages and across cultures.

A now iconic architectural marvel, the Cité du Vin is open to all. An innovative permanent, immersive, and sensory exhibition takes visitors through some twenty interactive, themed spaces covering 9,800 square feet (3,000 m^2) on the third floor. The impressively designed exhibit puts audiovisual and interactive experiences front and center, and wine is explored from every angle, whether it be history, geography, the arts, sciences, or flavors.

↑↗
Cité du Vin
134 Quai de Bacalan
33 300 Bordeaux
laciteduvin.com

Tickets include rental of the “Visit Companion,” a multimedia guide in eight languages, with options for children and disabled visitors.

The experience continues 115 feet (35 m) in the air, in the Belvédère: visitors are invited to taste a glass of wine from a selection of winemaking regions from around the world—including Bordeaux, of course—or to enjoy a glass of organic grape juice, while taking in panoramic views of the city.

In addition to temporary exhibitions, the Cité regularly offers introductory tasting experiences and workshops to learn more about Bordeaux wines. These are held on the second floor, in circular rooms, where the friendly atmosphere encourages conversation and exchange. Visit the museum website to learn more.

A boutique, a wine cellar, restaurants, and a garden with free access complete the museum’s cultural offerings. The Cité du Vin—which was named by *National Geographic* as one of the seven most beautiful museums in the world—is a veritable hub, where it is easy to while away an afternoon strolling the grounds, relaxing, or having a bite to eat.

The online library offers access to a wealth of resources, including virtual visits, podcasts, online events, and videos, making Cité du Vin content accessible anywhere, any time.

Musée d’Aquitaine

This beautiful museum retraces the history of Bordeaux and the Aquitaine region, from prehistory to the present day. A themed exhibition introduces visitors to the history of Bordeaux wine through the museum’s collections, and attests to the essential role of wine and the wine trade.

Bordeaux’s location, on the banks of the Garonne River and in proximity to the ocean, makes it particularly suited to trade. Protohistoric records show that wine was imported to Aquitaine from Italy, Spain, and Greece. During Antiquity, Burdigala became the center of a prosperous region by virtue of its winemaking activity. First amphoras, then casks were used to preserve and transport wine.

In the Middle Ages, Anglo-Gasconne Guyenne exported massively to England and Northern Europe. In the eighteenth century, a portion of the region's production was sent to the West Indies, where many residents of Bordeaux settled. In the nineteenth century, Bordeaux's châteaux were booming and the port asserted its role in trade, giving the region access to the world via the maritime routes.

Of particular interest are Jean Dupas's magnificent monumental art deco canvas, *La Vigne et le Vin* (Vine and Wine); Raoul Larche's bas-relief of a bacchante (created around 1910), depicting a young woman as an allegory of the vineyard's generosity and surrounded by the inscription "*Je ris, je chante, vive le vin*" (I laugh, I sing, long live wine); and the rare older pieces, including a pewterware pitcher from Bordeaux that was used as an official unit of measure in the late seventeenth century.

Musée d'Aquitaine
20 Cours Pasteur
33 000 Bordeaux
musee-aquitaine-bordeaux.fr

Musée National des Douanes (National Customs Museum)

Discover the unique history of one of the oldest branches of the French civil service, which has been tasked with managing and inspecting the country's winemaking industry since the Roman Empire. The museum's collections of artefacts and artwork retrace the influence of economic theories over the centuries and the various strategies used in the fight against smuggling, as well as the development of external trade and transport.

"A bottle of wine contains more philosophy than all the books in the world." —LOUIS PASTEUR

Musée National des Douanes
1 Place de la Bourse
33 000 Bordeaux
musee-douanes.fr

The only one of its kind in France, the museum is housed in a former customs hall in the Hôtel des Fermes du Roy, the precursor to the country's modern-day customs department. The building was originally home to the Ferme Générale, a private company that collected taxes for the king under the ancien régime. The Hôtel is intimately tied to the city's development and trade: it was the gateway for merchandise transported by ship and offloaded in the customs hall, where it was inspected by the Ferme's civil servants in order to replenish the kingdom's coffers. Inside, the hall with its beautiful arches extends for an impressive 131 feet (40 m).

With its global, borderless perspective, this museum offers a varied year-round program that is centered particularly on major international, national, and local cultural events, and includes concerts, readings, and performances. The museum's temporary exhibitions give visitors the opportunity to learn more about topics presented in the permanent collections or to explore new themes.

The Centre de Documentation Historique welcomes researchers, journalists, and customs history enthusiasts. The library contains more than six thousand documents and houses a picture library with over twenty-six thousand images.

Institut Culturel Bernard Magrez (ICBM)

Bernard Magrez—owner of four crus classés (including Château La Tour Carnet and Clos Haut Peraguey), as well as several other vineyards in the south of France and eight other countries—needs no introduction. A native of Bordeaux, he established this endowment fund to support artists and provide broad access to contemporary artistic creation.

Bridging tradition and innovation, this institute is a private, philanthropic artistic initiative driven by Magrez's desire to share his enthusiasm for art and artists. Today, it is one of the leading centers of contemporary art and street art in the Aquitaine region.

The institute's missions are to promote access to contemporary artworks for all audiences, through the creation or

QUINCONCES

This sprawling esplanade, where the annual Fête du Vin is held, features several sculptures, including the *Monument aux Girondins*: a tribute to the Girondists, topped with a winged statue representing Liberty. When the sculpture was restored in 2005, a coin bearing the effigy of Napoleon III, dated 1855, was discovered under the winged statue, a symbolic way to date the monument's construction. A silver coin stamped with the year of the restoration and commemorating the 150th anniversary of the 1855 classification was minted by the Monnaie de Paris (Paris Mint) and placed alongside the original coin, under the statue, to mark the occasion.

BORDEAUX IN NUMBERS

9TH
LARGEST CITY
in France, with
250,000 INHABITANTS

5TH LARGEST
URBAN AREA
in France,
comprising **28 COMMUNES**
and around **800,000 INHABITANTS**

¾ OF A MILE
(1.2 KM)
The longest pedestrian avenue in Europe: **RUE SAINTE-CATHERINE**

253 FT. (77 M) HIGH
AND 1,886 FT. (575 M) LONG
The highest and longest vertical-lift bridge in Europe:
PONT CHABAN DELMAS

29,000 ACRES
(117,500 HA)
The largest fine winegrowing region in the world

The largest number of
RESTAURANTS
per inhabitant in France

53 MILES
(86 KM)
The longest regional tramway network in France

427 FT. (130 M) LONG
AND 130 FT. (42 M) WIDE
The largest urban reflecting pool in the world:
PLACE DE LA BOURSE

SOURCE
Office de Tourisme et de Congrès de Bordeaux Métropole

Institut Culturel Bernard Magrez
16 Rue de Tivoli
33 000 Bordeaux
institut-bernard-magrez.com

promotion of cultural events, to support artistic endeavors, and to aid the production of new works by setting up residences with workshops for young artists and awarding artistic prizes.

ICBM has three exhibition spaces: the Château, which accommodates large-scale exhibitions of international artists (Seth, JonOne, and Rancinan are several recent examples); the Pavillon de la Boétie, where each year several nationally known French artists, who also receive support for their creative process from the institute, are exhibited; and the Galerie des Nouveaux Talents, where emerging artists can exhibit their work and gain recognition among a wider audience.

ICBM regularly hosts classical music concerts and the Nuits du Savoir conference series that gives Bordeaux residents access to high-level cultural events offered by nationally recognized speakers on current topics.

"Wine is the intellectual part of a meal, while meat and vegetables are merely the substance." —ALEXANDRE DUMAS

THE WINES

THE 1855 CLASSIFICATION OF BORDEAUX WINES

"When it comes to wine, you have to know how to put pleasure before prestige." —**PAUL CLAUDEL**

MORE THAN A NETWORK

GLOBAL WINE AMBASSADORSHIP

Established by the Chambre de Commerce et d'Industrie Bordeaux Gironde (Bordeaux Gironde Chamber of Commerce) on the occasion of the Paris World's Fair, the 1855 Classification is an internationally renowned ranking that recognizes Bordeaux's most prestigious grands crus. A library located within the chamber of commerce building, at Place de la Bourse, is dedicated to members of the classification.

From the promotion of the jewel in Bordeaux's crown, to networking and training industry professionals, the CCI Bordeaux Gironde has always shown active support for this esteemed sector, which has made Bordeaux famous around the world. It also helps to organize international events such as the Vinexposium fairs (formerly Vinexpo wine and spirits fairs), in which it is a stockholder. CCI Bordeaux Gironde also initiated in 1999 the Great Wine Capitals Global Network to foster commercial, touristic, and educational exchanges between its members, from Adelaide to Napa

Valley. Since 2004, CCI Bordeaux Gironde and the network have organized the Best of Wine Tourism award, which encourages the development of high-quality wine tourism. Finally, CCI Bordeaux Gironde also established the Kedge Wine School, an international reference in education for future managers in the wine and spirits sector.
Patrick Seguin, president of the CCI Bordeaux Gironde

History

The first classification of food products in the world owes its existence to an old rivalry between France and England. The World's Fair organized by Emperor Napoleon III in 1855 was the French response to a similar event held in London four years earlier. Whereas England celebrated the Industrial Revolution, which had forced a large portion of its rural population to leave its land, France chose, belatedly but significantly, to highlight its most famous area of agricultural excellence: winemaking.

Following common practice at international fairs, the wines sent in from different regions of France had to be tasted by a jury. Of this tasting only an amusing anecdote survives: the unfinished bottles were sent to the cafeterias of Paris' hospitals "to revive the ill, unaccustomed to Château-Lafite wines," according to Mr. Saint-Amant. The jury's winners were overshadowed by a history-making classification: the 1855 grands crus.

To prepare for the World's Fair in record time, the Bordeaux Chamber of Commerce was tasked with organizing "a complete and satisfying presentation of the department's wines." The Chamber president collected six bottles from each estate. For the sake of fairness, he had standardized labels created by the Chamber of Commerce, which were printed with the names of the château, town, and owner, added to each bottle. He then asked the Broker's Union, located near the Bordeaux stock exchange, to provide a "list of all the red classed-growths in the department" and "the classification regarding white wines."

The brokers were the ideal choice for the job, since they managed to avoid the power struggles that pitted merchants against estate owners. They also had the best overall understanding of wine production and were as familiar with production techniques as they were with the workings of the trade. Moreover, their status as ministerial officers bound them to a certain level of integrity.

The classification was not based on a tasting: the Brokers' Union and its deputies carried out a statistical analysis based on historical prices of 900-liter (238-gallon) casks produced by the estates. Inevitably, there were objections, but the fact remains: the classification was a landmark moment and the happy representatives of this "cork aristocracy" have endured over the years, their reputations intact, despite the ebb and flow of crises and trends.

The 1855 Classification in no way negates its competitors' merits, but, for the last 167 years, it has been the only historic selection, comprising some of the most beautiful estates in the world, as Philippe Castéja, president of the Conseil des Grands Crus Classés de 1855, so accurately sums up: "It is an incredible challenge. It forces us to stay in the lead and remain the front runner. It is an incredible history that no one else can lay claim to."

"Wine is a kind of internal cosmetic that beautifies, for an instant, the face of our thoughts." —HENRI DE RÉGNIER

THE PERILS OF POWDERY MILDEW

In 1852, twenty years before the appearance of phylloxera, powdery mildew—a parasite that arrived from England—contaminated a large portion of the Médoc vineyards. The severe crisis mobilized wine professionals at every level: producers, civil servants, and scientists worked together but struggled to determine the nature and origin of the problem. They tried, unsuccessfully, to clean the vines with water, soot, and chloride, before sulfur was discovered to be effective, and, around 1860, the Compte de la Vergne, an estate owner in Ludon-Médoc, developed a bellows system that eradicated the scourge. This marked the beginning of a golden age for winemakers in Bordeaux.

ETHICAL CHARTER

The Conseil des Grands Crus Classés 1855 adopted a sustainable excellence charter intended to enhance its terroir, protect its heritage and the well-being of its employees, and ensure respect for biodiversity. The charter is based on the ISO 26.000 norm and respects Social Corporate Responsibility criteria.
WEBSITE gcc-1855.fr/charte-ethique/

KEY FIGURES

87 CHÂTEAUX

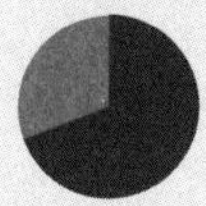

60 REDS
(59 Médoc and 1 Graves)
on 9,884 acres (4,000 ha)

27 SWEET WHITES
(17 Sauternes and 10 Barsac)
on 29,000 acres (1,200 ha)

EUROPEAN AND WORLDWIDE RECOGNITION

The prestigious nature of this historic classification is protected by the Conseil des Grands Crus Classés 1855, which has fought against all forms of misappropriation since its creation. The classification is recognized by the European Union. Since 2015, the date "1855" has been accepted as a traditional European wine term, as are the terms "château," "premier cru," and "cru classé." The brand name "Grand Cru Classé 1855" is recognized in China and protected by copyright.
WEBSITE gcc-1855.fr/

WINE IS ONE OF THE MOST CIVILIZED THINGS IN THE WORLD.

—ERNEST HEMINGWAY

KEY DATES

325
The poet Ausonius, born around 309 CE in Aquitaine, mentions the vineyards of Médoc and his love of Pauillac in his letters to Theon.

1137
Eleanor of Aquitaine marries Louis VII of France.

1152
Eleanor of Aquitaine marries Henry Plantagenet, Duke of Anjou and future king of England, marking the beginning of three hundred years of English rule in Bordeaux.

1453
Battle of Castillon. English general John Talbot loses the battle and the French Crown reclaims Aquitaine.

1584
Michel de Montaigne, mayor of Bordeaux, receives Henry of Navarre, the future Henry IV, who would later bring engineers from the Netherlands to drain the marshes of Médoc.

1666
Following the Great Fire of London, the Pontac family purchases a tavern and names it Pontac's Head. Haut-Brion, the family's wine, is served there and establishes the château's reputation. Pontac's Head becomes the most fashionable eating house in London.

1755
Bordeaux wine is served at Versailles. Louis XV suffers from intestinal troubles for which the Duke of Richelieu prescribes "Lafite." The cru becomes the preferred wine of the king and the entire royal court. The reputation of Bordeaux "medicine" is established.

1778
The first United States consular post is established in Bordeaux in March 1778.

1787
Thomas Jefferson, the United States Ambassador to France and future third president of the United States of America, takes a five-day trip to Bordeaux in May 1787. He compiles a classification of Bordeaux wines very similar to that established in 1855.

1855
At the request of Emperor Napoleon III, the classification of Bordeaux wines is published on the occasion of the Paris World's Fair.

1875
Phylloxera ravages Bordeaux's vineyards.

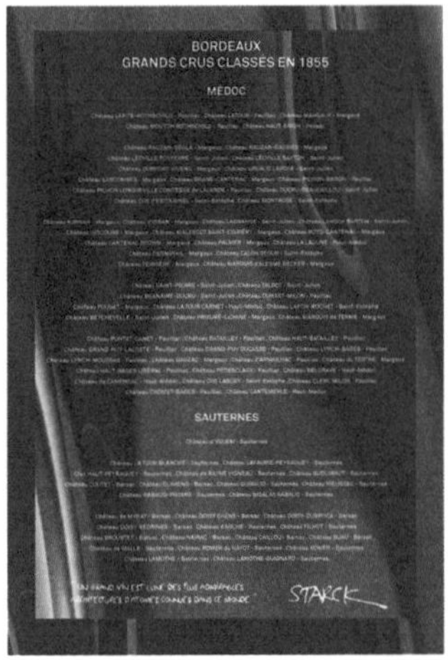

1988

The exhibition *Bordeaux Châteaux* is held at the Centre Georges Pompidou in Paris from November 16, 1988 through February 1989. The English architectural painter Carl Laubin has the idea of bringing together on one canvas all sixty-one Médoc grands crus from the famous 1855 Classification. The work is sold at auction in New York in 1991.

2005

The 150th anniversary of the 1855 Classification of Bordeaux Wines is included in the French ministry of culture's list of national celebrations. A commemorative coin is minted by the Monnaie de Paris (Paris Mint) with the approval of the minister of economy. Flammarion publishes a book that retraces the history of the classification; an incredible success, it is translated into eight languages.

2008

The renowned photographer Yann Arthus-Bertrand emphasizes the human touch behind the 1855 grands crus classés in a poster that meets with immediate international success; thousands of copies are distributed in fifty or so countries.

2015

The 160th anniversary of the 1855 Classification is celebrated at the ministry of foreign affairs (Quai d'Orsay, Paris) on April 20, 2015, by the minister Laurent Fabius and the secretary of state for foreign trade and tourism Mattias Fekel. In December, a tasting is held at the European Parliament in Brussels to commemorate the achievement of obtaining copyright protection in a wine context for the number "1855."

2019

One of France's leading designers, Philippe Starck, combines his artistic vision with great wines to design a new poster featuring the names of the grands crus classés. As he declares, "A great wine is one of the most admirable constructions of atoms known to man."

↖

Detail of the poster by Yann Arthus-Bertrand, 2008

↑

Poster by Philippe Starck, 2019

→

Painting by Carl Laubin for the exhibition *Bordeaux Châteaux*, 1988

MÉDOC GRANDS CRUS IN THE 1855 CLASSIFICATION

PREMIERS CRUS

Château Lafite-Rothschild
PAUILLAC 1

Château Latour
PAUILLAC 2

Château Margaux
MARGAUX 3

Château Mouton Rothschild
PAUILLAC 4

Château Haut-Brion
PESSAC 5

DEUXIÈMES CRUS

Château Rauzan-Ségla
MARGAUX 6

Château Rauzan-Gassies
MARGAUX 7

Château Léoville-Poyferré
SAINT-JULIEN 8

Château Léoville Barton
SAINT-JULIEN 9

Château Durfort-Vivens
MARGAUX 10

Château Gruaud Larose
SAINT-JULIEN 11

Château Lascombes
MARGAUX 12

Château Brane-Cantenac
MARGAUX 13

Château Pichon Baron
PAUILLAC 14

Château Pichon Longueville Comtesse de Lalande
PAUILLAC 15

Château Ducru-Beaucaillou
SAINT-JULIEN 16

Château Cos d'Estournel
SAINT-ESTÈPHE 17

Château Montrose
SAINT-ESTÈPHE 18

TROISIÈMES CRUS

Château Kirwan
MARGAUX 19

Château d'Issan
MARGAUX 20

Château Lagrange
SAINT-JULIEN 21

Château Langoa Barton
SAINT-JULIEN 22

Château Giscours
MARGAUX 23

Château Malescot Saint-Exupéry
MARGAUX 24

Château Boyd-Cantenac
MARGAUX 25

Château Cantenac Brown
MARGAUX 26

Château Palmer
MARGAUX 27

Château la Lagune
HAUT-MÉDOC 28

Château Desmirail
MARGAUX 29

Château Calon Ségur
SAINT-ESTÈPHE 30

Château Ferrière
MARGAUX 31

Château Marquis d'Alesme Becker
MARGAUX 32

QUATRIÈMES CRUS

Château Saint-Pierre
SAINT-JULIEN 33

Château Talbot
SAINT-JULIEN 34

Château Branaire-Ducru
SAINT-JULIEN 35

Château Duhart-Milon
PAUILLAC 36

Château Pouget
MARGAUX 37

Château La Tour Carnet
HAUT-MÉDOC 38

Château Lafon-Rochet
SAINT-ESTÈPHE 39

Château Beychevelle
SAINT-JULIEN 40

Château Prieuré-Lichine
MARGAUX 41

Château Marquis de Terme
MARGAUX 42

CINQUIÈMES CRUS

Château Pontet-Canet
PAUILLAC 43

Château Batailley
PAUILLAC 44

Château Haut-Batailley
PAUILLAC 45

Château Grand-Puy-Lacoste
PAUILLAC 46

Château Grand-Puy Ducasse
PAUILLAC 47

Château Lynch-Bages
PAUILLAC 48

Château Lynch-Moussas
PAUILLAC 49

Château Dauzac
MARGAUX 50

Château d'Armailhac
PAUILLAC 51

Château du Tertre
MARGAUX 52

Château Haut-Bages Libéral
PAUILLAC 53

Château Pédesclaux
PAUILLAC 54

Château Belgrave
HAUT-MÉDOC 55

Château de Camensac
HAUT-MÉDOC 56

Château Cos Labory
SAINT-ESTÈPHE 57

Château Clerc Milon
PAUILLAC 58

Château Croizet-Bages
PAUILLAC 59

Château Cantemerle
HAUT-MÉDOC 60

SAUTERNES AND BARSAC GRANDS CRUS IN THE 1855 CLASSIFICATION

PREMIER CRU SUPÉRIEUR

Château d'Yquem
SAUTERNES 61
AOC SAUTERNES

PREMIER CRU

Château la Tour Blanche
SAUTERNES 62

Château Lafaurie-Peyraguey
SAUTERNES 63

Clos Haut-Peyraguey
SAUTERNES 64

Château de Rayne Vigneau
SAUTERNES 65

Château Suduiraut
SAUTERNES 66

Château Coutet
BARSAC 67

Château Climens
BARSAC 68

Château Guiraud
SAUTERNES 69

Château Rieussec
SAUTERNES 70

Château Rabaud-Promis
SAUTERNES 71

Château Sigalas Rabaud
SAUTERNES 72

DEUXIÈMES CRUS

Château de Myrat
BARSAC 73

Château Doisy Daëne
BARSAC 74

Château Doisy-Dubroca
BARSAC 75

Château Doisy-Védrines
BARSAC 76

Château d'Arche
SAUTERNES 77

Château Filhot
SAUTERNES 78

Château Broustet
BARSAC 79

Château Nairac
BARSAC 80

Château Caillou
BARSAC 81

Château Suau
BARSAC 82

Château de Malle
SAUTERNES 83

Château Romer du Hayot
SAUTERNES 84

Château Romer
SAUTERNES 85

Château Lamothe
SAUTERNES 86

Château Lamothe-Guignard
SAUTERNES 87

RED WINES

9,390 ACRES

(3,800 HA)
surface area of the GCC red wine vineyards

6 APPELLATIONS D'ORIGINE CONTRÔLÉE

SAINT-ESTÈPHE, PAUILLAC, SAINT-JULIEN, MARGAUX, HAUT-MÉDOC, AND GRAVES

60 CRUS

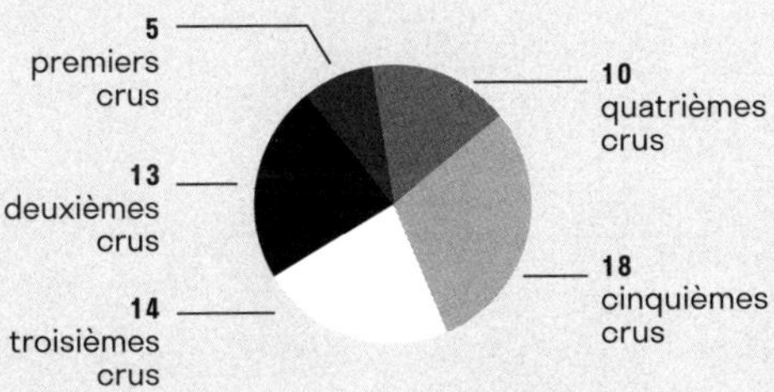

GCC BY APPELLATION

5 GCC in the Saint-Estèphe appellation
18 GCC in the Pauillac appellation
10 GCC in the Saint-Julien appellation
21 GCC in the Margaux appellation
5 GCC in the Haut-Médoc appellation
1 GCC in the Graves appellation

SWEET WHITE WINES

2,718 ACRES

(1,100 HA)
surface area of the GCC sweet white wine vineyards

2 APPELLATIONS D'ORIGINE CONTRÔLÉE

SAUTERNES AND BARSAC

27 CRUS

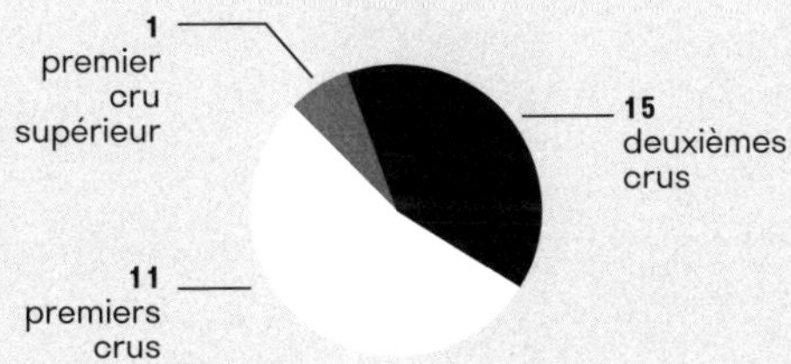

GCC BY APPELLATION

17 GCC in the Sauternes appellation
10 GCC in the Barsac appellation

THE WINE TRAVEL GUIDE

A TOUR OF THE CHÂTEAUX

"The splendor of Bordeaux's *grands vins* is not to be found in some extravagance, but in their well-balanced character—a classic, understated balance."

—**FRANCK FERRAND**

€: LESS THAN €10 ($11/£8) — **€€:** €10–€20 ($11–$22/£8–£17) — **€€€:** €20–€50 ($22–$55/£17–£42) — **€€€€:** €50+ ($55/£42)
($ and £ conversions, calculated at time of going to press, are approximate)
Estimated travel times provided by châteaux; check traffic conditions before travel.

DISCOVER THE FINE RED WINES

MÉDOC

Médoc is both a world-renowned winegrowing region that stretches along the Gironde estuary and a region featuring a wealth of diverse landscapes: the marshes of Bas-Médoc; long, fine sandy beaches on the coast; the Landes forest; and the Courdouan lighthouse at the Pointe de Grave, where the Gironde meets the Atlantic Ocean. In addition to its wines, a rich tradition of local cuisine based on the natural abundance of sea, river, and land is to be found in the Médoc region, as well as an extraordinary historical heritage.

GIRONDE
CHÂTEAU FERRIÈRE
3
12
D2
32
CHÂTEAU MALESCOT SAINT-EXUPÉRY
CHÂTEAU DUFORT-VIVENS
42
CHÂTEAU RAUZAN-GASSIES
CHÂTEAU RAUZAN-SÉGLA
CHÂTEAU PALMER
20
41
29
19
26
CHÂTEAU BOYD-CANTENAC
CHÂTEAU DAUZAC
13
CHÂTEAU POUGET
52
23
0
1km
½ mile

MÉDOC

MARGAUX

3 Château Margaux
23 Château Giscours
52 Château du Tertre
29 Château Desmirail
19 Château Kirwan
41 Château Prieuré-Lichine
20 Château d'Issan
13 Château Brane-Cantenac
26 Château Cantenac Brown
42 Château Marquis de Terme
32 Château Marquis d'Alesme Becker
12 Château Lascombes

3

CHÂTEAU MARGAUX

PREMIER GRAND CRU CLASSÉ, MARGAUX

A legendary wine

Château Margaux reflects the grandeur and fragility of destiny. Its history is marked by the families who have lived there and the vagaries of nature. For more than four centuries, the innovations of some and the talent of others—and, most importantly, a passion shared by all—have steadily made the wines of Château Margaux a byword for excellence. In the late seventeenth century, the estate was included among an emerging elite of "Premiers Crus," long before it was recognized in the official 1855 classification. Following in the footsteps of her father, who passed away in 1980, Corinne Mentzelopoulos now guides the future of Château Margaux.

GETTING THERE

Château Margaux is located about nineteen miles (30 km) north of Bordeaux, or a forty-minute drive on the D2 (Bordeaux Wine Route) or D209 highways.

ADDRESS

Château Margaux
33 460 Margaux-Cantenac
CONTACT
+33 (0)5 57 88 83 83
chateau-margaux.com

VINEYARD

The Château Margaux vineyard includes 215 acres (87 ha) of red grapes (75 percent Cabernet Sauvignon, 20 percent Merlot, 5 percent Petit Verdot and Cabernet Franc) and 27 acres (11 ha) of white grapes (100 percent Sauvignon Blanc). The vineyard is located on primarily gravel soil, but also includes clay and limestone soils. This diversity is partly responsible for the great complexity of the wines produced here.

TOURS & TASTINGS

Visits by appointment only.

215 ACRES

(87 ha) of vines

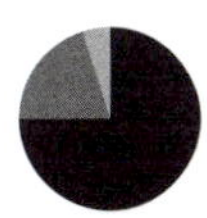

75% Cabernet Sauvignon
20% Merlot
5% Petit Verdot and Cabernet Franc

23

CHÂTEAU GISCOURS

TROISIÈME GRAND CRU CLASSÉ, MARGAUX

More than a wine—an experience
At Château Giscours, the pleasures of wine can be enjoyed in enchanting surroundings; the estate is home to a magnificent park embellished with water features, sculptures, and many rare tree varieties, including monkey puzzle, giant sequoia, and black oak. Here, just twelve miles (20 km) from Bordeaux, you will also find a working farm, complete with an impressive vegetable garden and pastureland dotted with Landais sheep and several breeds of Bordelaise cattle.

GETTING THERE

Château Giscours is located on the Bordeaux Wine Route (D2 highway), between the towns of Macau and Labarde, less than twelve miles (20 km) from Bordeaux.

ADDRESS

Château Giscours
10 Route de Giscours
33 460 Labarde

CONTACT
+33 (0)3 37 97 09 09
giscours.com/en/

SIGNATURE

This vast estate, untouched by time, is located on the site of a fourteenth-century fortified keep; the vineyard was planted two centuries later by a rich draper named Pierre de Lhomme. The château has changed hands many times over the centuries, with each new owner making their own novel contribution.

During the Second Empire (1852–70), the Count of Pescatore, a Parisian banker, went to great lengths to beautify the residence in preparation for a visit from Empress Eugénie. Later, between 1875 and 1890, the winegrower Édouard Cruse modernized the property and oversaw the creation of a park around the château. He also founded a model farm that he named after his wife, Suzanne. In 1952, Nicolas and Pierre Tari purchased the château and added the magnificent artificial lake. Eric Albada Jelgersma acquired the château in 1995 and made significant investments. Today, it is managed by his children, Dennis, Derk, and Valérie.

VINEYARD

This 247-acre (100-ha) vineyard extends over four gravelly knolls and is planted with roughly two-thirds Cabernet Sauvignon and one-third Merlot, with smaller amounts of Cabernet Franc and Petit Verdot, in keeping with the classic elegance specific to this grand cru classé.

A MERMAID WITH A SURPRISING HISTORY

The mermaid depicted on the label of this grand cru (and who lends its name to one of the château's wines) appeared in the early twentieth century. Its origins can be traced to the coat of arms of a prestigious Irish clan, the O'Byrnes. A member of the clan was among the many Jacobites who were forced to flee Ireland after the Battle of Aughrim in 1691. He built the neighboring château, La Houringue, where the mermaid featured as a decorative element and inspired Émile Grange, who had just acquired Giscours.

TOURS & TASTINGS

Open Tour of the Grounds
This affordably priced tour includes a glass of the estate's wine, and the option to book a gourmet cheese and charcuterie platter. Immerse yourself in the unspoiled nature of Giscours's park and forest, where you will encounter a variety of rare trees and protected flora, as well as works of art superbly incorporated into this natural setting.

Private Tours
Two private tours of the château are available upon reservation, with or without a golf cart tour of the winery. The number of wines and vintages included in the tasting can be personalized.
DURATION 2 hours
PRICE €€€€

FOOD & DRINK/ CHÂTEAU STAYS

Picnic in the Park
The estate grounds are open to strollers, but those who wish to picnic in style can book a gourmet hamper containing a selection of local and homemade produce, as well as a glass of the château's wine, all served alfresco with a flourish. This accessible option is a relaxed yet epicurean way to discover the château.
PRICE €€€€

For Groups
The château offers a lunch and dinner service featuring light or gastronomic menus created from first-rate farm produce.
PRICE €€€€

Guest Rooms
Château Giscours has three charming guest rooms located in the Old Stables, overlooking the vineyards.
PRICE €€€€

52

CHÂTEAU DU TERTRE

CINQUIÈME GRAND CRU CLASSÉ, MARGAUX

Evolving traditions
The history of this estate dates to the sixteenth century, when Thomas de Montaigne, brother of French philosopher Michel de Montaigne, married Jacquette d'Arsac and, in 1590, became lord of the noble houses Arsac and Castéra in Médoc. A long list of prestigious owners followed, including the Marquis de Ségur, whom Louis XV christened Prince of the Vines.

GETTING THERE

Château du Tertre is located about nineteen miles (30 km) north of Bordeaux, or a forty-minute drive away.

ADDRESS

Château du Tertre
14 Allée du Tertre
33 460 Arsac

CONTACT

reservations@chateaudutertre.fr
chateaudutertre.fr

ARCHITECTURE

The main building, a mid-eighteenth-century *chartreuse*, was built at the request of Pierre Mitchell, an Irish merchant and founder of the first glass-bottle factory in Bordeaux.

In 1997, after a difficult period, Dutch businessman Eric Albada Jelgersma bought the estate and made considerable investments to completely restructure the technical facilities. He restored the *chartreuse* to its original symmetrical appearance by building a wing based on the eighteenth-century floor plans. He also added a magnificent tree-filled garden, a water feature, and an orangery to the property.

SIGNATURE

The château uses different types of vats during the winemaking process, including wood vats that bring out the silky mouthfeel typical of Margaux wines, and an oval, concrete vat specially designed to reproduce the internal movement of ancient amphoras. This keeps the dregs suspended in the liquid and contributes roundness to the wine. The Helfrich family took over in March 2021 and continues to uphold the legendary reputation of Château du Tertre.

VINEYARD

Unchanged since 1855, the vineyard covers 143 uninterrupted acres (58 ha) on one of the highest hilltops in Arsac, in the Médoc region. Here, as elsewhere, Gunzian gravel plays a role in temperature regulation by accumulating heat during the day and releasing it at night, which protects the vineyard from late spring frosts. The relatively high proportion of Cabernet Blanc (over a quarter) reflects the rich, spicy character of this grand cru classé.

TOURS & TASTINGS

In the Footsteps of Château du Tertre
In addition to the guided tour to discover the estate's history, winemaking techniques, and charming private garden, you'll taste the grand cru and two other wines, Tertre Blanc and Hauts du Tertre.
DURATION 1½ hours
TASTING 3 wines
PRICE €€

The Private Tour
After learning the secrets of Château du Tertre during a private visit, you will be served a glass of Tertre Blanc in an intimate setting, before your guide takes you on a journey through time via a vertical tasting of three great vintages of this grand cru classé.
DURATION 2 hours
TASTING 4 wines
PRICE €€

Picnic in the Park
This mouthwatering option is offered on sunny days (for groups of at least two and up to ten). Following a guided visit of the winemaking facilities, you'll be invited to taste a vintage of Château du Tertre, before enjoying a picnic of local, homemade produce on the estate's grounds.
PRICE €€€€

FOOD & DRINK/ CHÂTEAU STAYS

Château du Tertre offers five delightful guest rooms, all overlooking the vineyard, that were tastefully decorated by renowned Belgian interior designer Axel Vervoordt.

143 ACRES
(58 ha) of vines

45
C 14 PV
2013
le 17.3.2015
35 hl

29

CHÂTEAU DESMIRAIL

TROISIÈME GRAND CRU CLASSÉ, MARGAUX

Drinkable works of art

This château was founded in the mid-eighteenth century by Marguerite Rauzan du Ribail and was named after her husband, the future president of the Bordeaux Parliament. The estate slipped into obscurity on the eve of World War II, when its brand name and a large portion of its land were acquired by Château Palmer, who kept the vines but sold off the buildings. However, Lucien Lurton endeavored to piece the original vineyard back together through a series of purchases and exchanges, establishing it in the heart of Cantenac in 1980 and restoring the old buildings, including a typical eighteenth-century *chartreuse*. Twelve years later, he passed Château Desmirail on to one of his sons, Denis.

GETTING THERE

In the commune of Margaux-Cantenac, in the southeastern area of the Margaux appellation, the entrance to Château Desmirail is the first on the Bordeaux Wine Route (D2 highway), less than nineteen miles (30 km) from Bordeaux.

ADDRESS

Château Desmirail
28 Avenue de la 5e République
33 460 Margaux-Cantenac

CONTACT

+33 (0)5 57 88 34 33
desmirail.com

CHÂTEAU
DESMIRAIL

VISION

Denis Lurton continues to pursue his father's vision, convinced that "wine is born from the union of nature and culture; it is at once the fruit of the vine, of the terroir, and of the work of men over the centuries."

VINEYARD

This estate—with eighty-seven acres (35 ha) in the Margaux appellation and twelve acres (5 ha) in the Haut-Médoc—has some twenty plots (the majority of which belonged to the vineyard in the nineteenth century) spread over the towns of Arsac, Margaux-Cantenac, and Soussans. They are planted with 50 percent Cabernet Sauvignon, 40 percent Merlot, 5 percent Cabernet Franc, and 5 percent Petit Verdot on a terroir of deep gravelly soil.

99 ACRES
(40 ha) of vines

87 ACRES (35 HA)
in the Margaux appellation
12 ACRES (5 HA)
in the Haut-Médoc appellation

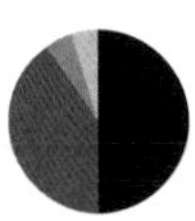

50% Cabernet Sauvignon
40% Merlot
5% Cabernet Franc
5% Petit Verdot

SIGNATURE

In 1997, Denis Lurton installed ten new thermoregulated fermenting vats; two years later, he replaced the old wooden vats used to vinify the oldest plots. At the same time, he carried out a rejuvenation of the vines, focusing on the four chosen grape varieties. The château uses sustainable winegrowing practices, having abandoned all use of chemical weed control and insecticides decades ago. These efforts have earned Château Desmirail its High Environmental Value certification, held since the production of its 2018 vintage. The wine is aged in oak barrels for a year. During this time, the barrels are regularly topped up, to compensate for loss from absorption or evaporation, and racked, to separate the clear wine from the lees. About half of the wine is aged in new barrels and the other half in older barrels. At the end of this maturing period, the wine is blended in vats, where it undergoes a final clarification known as fining.

The resulting wine is typical of the Margaux appellation: well-balanced, soft, and velvety, with a finesse and elegance that have earned it a growing reputation. It is a truly "drinkable work of art," as Denis Lurton beautifully describes it.

TOURS & TASTINGS

Classic Tour
During this tour, you will learn about the wine classification, the region's vineyards, the history of the château, the Lurton family, and vinification and aging methods. The tour culminates with a tasting of three of the château's wines.
DURATION 1 hour
TASTING 3 wines
PRICE €

Wine and Cheese Tour
Following a tour of the property, epicureans can explore the flavors of six varieties of cheese specially selected to pair perfectly with Château Desmirail and the estate's other wines.
DURATION 1½ hours
TASTING 3 wines and 6 cheeses
PRICE €€

Olfactory Tour
After a visit to the wine cellars, put your olfactory skills to the test and try to identify the different notes to be found in the barrels and wines.
DURATION 1½ hours
TASTING 3 wines
PRICE €€

19

CHÂTEAU KIRWAN

TROISIÈME GRAND CRU CLASSÉ, MARGAUX

Pure Margaux charm

Kirwan has one of those Gaelic-sounding names that recall Médoc's historic connection to Ireland. For many years, the château bore the name of its first owner, Renaud de La Salle, before being renamed in 1775 by Mark Kirwan, a native of Galway. Bordeaux wine merchant Camille Godard, who hailed from a family of botanists, designed the château's beautiful gardens and fishpond, dug the first artesian well in Médoc, planted the rose arbor, and commissioned the greenhouse and cellars. Since 1926, Château Kirwan has belonged to the Schÿlers, a family of wine merchants who settled in Bordeaux in 1739.

GETTING THERE

Château Kirwan is located in Cantenac, about nineteen miles (30 km) north of Bordeaux, or a forty-minute drive away.

ADDRESS

Château Kirwan
Chemin de Kirwan
33 460 Margaux-Cantenac

CONTACT

+33 (0)5 57 88 71 00
mail@chateau-kirwan.com
chateau-kirwan.com

94 ACRES
(38 ha) of vines

VISION

For more than a decade, Château Kirwan has demonstrated its firm commitment to sustainable development and spares no effort in striving to preserve its terroir and resources. Soils are maintained without the use of herbicides and vineyard treatments have been reduced by half over the last ten years, earning this grand cru classé the prestigious Level 3 High Environmental Value certification by the French Ministry of Agriculture in 2017.
All the while, the château continues to express the refinement, charm, and depth unique to Margaux's terroir.

INNOVATION AND DESIGN

The château's winemaking facilities were entirely renovated between 2015 and 2017. Thirty-seven custom-made concrete fermenting vats were added, in addition to a new first-year cellar connecting the fermenting room to the existing cellars. Visitors to the château are greeted by the cellar's incredible steel facade, created by the Russian artists Anatoly and Kinga Stolnikoff, which depicts an impressive rootstock, at once hardy and delicate. Its lacy foliage conceals a bouquet of words evoking the property, its history, and the countless qualities of its wine.

VINEYARD

The ninety-four-acre (38 ha) vineyard is dominated by Cabernet Sauvignon (45 percent), cultivated on the precocious terroirs of the Cantenac plateau, where smaller parcels of Petit Verdot are also found. Merlot was transferred from soils rich in clay and replanted on sandier, slightly cooler parcels in order to limit alcohol levels. This also results in grapes with a freshness that contributes to the full-bodied, velvety character of these wines.

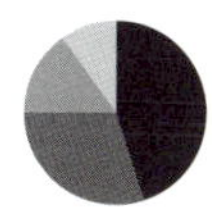

45% Cabernet Sauvignon
30% Merlot
15% Cabernet Franc
10% Petit Verdot

TOURS & TASTINGS

The following is a selection from Château Kirwan's particularly rich program of tastings and workshops.

The Short-Lived Tasting

Learn to unravel the secrets of a grand cru classé: after a guided visit of the property and cellars, a member of the winemaking team will teach you how to judge a wine's potential during aging and understand the complexity of this process.

DURATION 1½ hours
TASTING 2 wines
PRICE €€€

The Vintage-Year Tasting

During this original tour, you will have the opportunity to taste the vintage of your choice, whether it be your birth year, wedding year, or any other significant date. You will decant a bottle of the selected vintage, then taste it alongside a younger vintage in the wine cellar.

DURATION 1½ hours
TASTING 2 wines
PRICE €€€

The Prestigious Tour

This tour—a favorite with visitors—includes a precise, detailed presentation of winegrowing techniques and the château's winemaking philosophy. You'll start in the vineyard, then make your way to the wine cellar and fermenting room, before ending the visit in the château's gardens. The tour includes a tasting of the grand cru and Charmes de Kirwan.

DURATION 1 hour
TASTING 2 wines
PRICE €€€

A Gourmet Day in Margaux

Three châteaux have teamed up to give you an unforgettable introduction to all that Margaux has to offer. You will start the day at Château Prieuré-Lichine, where you'll learn about the history of the appellation and the 1855 classification—and, of course, taste the château's white wine, accompanied by a terrine of sturgeon caviar from Aquitaine. You'll then head to Château Kirwan, where you'll enjoy a picnic lunch and learn about the history of wine and the wine trade, followed by a blind tasting. For the third course, you'll learn about the art of blending at Château La Tour de Bessan, where you'll be presented with a selection of monovarietal wines accompanied by *sarments du Médoc*—local chocolates in the form of slender vine shoots.

DURATION 1 day
TASTING Wines from 3 châteaux and local produce
PRICE €€€€

WORKSHOPS

100 Percent Single Grapes

Play the role of apprentice oenologist during this workshop. You'll create your own wine on the astute advice of Château Kirwan's technical director. Taste grapes from three plots and learn to blend them to create a wine typical of Margaux.

DURATION 2½ hours
TASTING 2 wines
PRICE €€€€

Japanese Flavors

If you are looking for novel pairing ideas to surprise your friends or want to discover new flavors, then this is the workshop for you. Let Japanese chef Junko Sakurai be your guide, as he teaches you how to prepare different specialties like gyoza, soba noodles, and ginger fried chicken, and how to pair these dishes with a selection of Château Kirwan vintages.

DURATION 2½–3 hours
TASTING 2 wines
PRICE €€€€

FOOD & DRINK

What better way to taste a grand cru classé and make the most of your time in the region than by enjoying your wine with sweet or savory dishes prepared by local chef Sabrina Epelva? Reserve one of three options: picnic, brunch (May to October), or gourmet aperitif.

DURATION 1½ hours (picnic or aperitif); 2½ hours (brunch)
TASTING 1–2 wines

41

CHÂTEAU PRIEURÉ-LICHINE

QUATRIÈME GRAND CRU CLASSÉ, MARGAUX

Centuries of devotion

The history of this estate dates back to the Middle Ages, when the Priory of Cantenac was founded by the Benedictine monks of Vertheuil Abbey. This grand cru classé is therefore one of the oldest winegrowing properties in the region, and the only one whose roots do not lie in an aristocratic stronghold or a bourgeois residence. It wasn't until the early eighteenth century, after the historic frosts of 1709, that the entirety of the priory's crops, orchards, pastures, and forests were converted for winegrowing.

GETTING THERE

Château Prieuré-Lichine is located about nineteen miles (30 km) north of Bordeaux, or a forty-minute drive away.

ADDRESS

Château Prieuré-Lichine
34 Avenue de la 5e République
33 460 Margaux-Cantenac

CONTACT

+33 (0)5 57 88 36 28
prieure-lichine.fr

NAME

The château is named after Alexis Lichine, a prominent figure in the wine world and the renowned author of the *Encyclopedia of Wines and Spirits*. He acquired the château in 1951 and set about modernizing the existing facilities, rebuilding the former ecclesiastical residence, and progressively increasing the vineyard area, calling on Émile Peynaud—regarded as the father of modern oenology—for assistance.

SIGNATURE

In 1999, the Ballande family purchased the cru. They began to completely restructure the facilities in 2012: the harvest reception area was modernized to introduce gravity-flow in the vat-filling system, and thirty-four new concrete vats were installed. With capacities of 2,100–3,100 gallons (80–120 hl), the diverse vats enable a more precise plot-selection process. Gentle extraction is used during primary fermentation to bring out the rich, velvety tannic structure that is characteristic of this grand cru classé.

VINEYARD

Spread over four communes that make up the Margaux appellation, Château Prieuré-Lichine's parcel distribution is, in more ways than one, particularly representative of the appellation. The vineyard is harvested by hand and is planted on a terroir comprised of gravelly soil deposited during successive periods of deglaciation during the Quaternary period. Runoff then carved these sedimentary soils into well-drained hilltops facing the Gironde estuary.

WORKSHOPS

Test Your Wine-Tasting Powers
This fun, interactive workshop focuses on the art of tasting. Through a variety of activities, you will learn to engage your five senses and awaken the sommelier within.
DURATION 2 hours
PRICE €€€

Terroirs Beyond Borders
Escape into the vineyards of Bordeaux with this tasting of three to six wines representative of this winemaking region. You'll learn to appreciate the unique characteristics and personality of each wine as you sample one terroir after another.
DURATION 1–2 hours
TASTING 3–6 wines
PRICE €€€

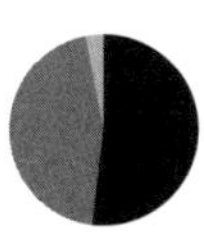

52% Merlot
45% Cabernet Sauvignon
3% Petit Verdot

TOURS & TASTINGS

The château is open year round, seven days a week during high season. In keeping with a long tradition of hospitality, it was among the first châteaux to provide a tasting room for guests, attracting wine enthusiasts from around the world to the Médoc region. For an additional fee, a sweet or savory food pairing can be added to all visits.

Discovery Tour
Discover the different stages in the production of a Margaux grand cru classé during a tour of the estate and its facilities. For the tasting, you may choose between several of the château's wines, including a small-run white wine.
DURATION 1½ hours
TASTING 1–3 wines
PRICE €

Private Tours
This option is ideal for couples and small groups, who can enjoy a customized tour adapted to their individual interests.
DURATION 1½ hours
PRICE €€

Historical Tour
Travel through more than five hundred years of history at the heart of the Margaux appellation, and immerse yourself in the Bordeaux wine adventure and the Imperial Classification of 1855. This tour ends with a tasting that includes two historically revealing vintages of Château Prieuré-Lichine.
DURATION 2 hours
TASTING 3 wines
PRICE €€

Terroir Tour
Deepen your knowledge of soils and *cépages* with a focus on varietals most representative of the appellation. You will also receive insightful explanations about the tasks performed in the vineyard and the concept of blending, before tasting several monovarietal and blended wines from different terroirs.
DURATION 2 hours
TASTING 4 wines
PRICE €€

"Saveur" Tour
This tour will introduce you to different tasting techniques through a series of practical exercises. You will also learn the basics of serving wine and how to form the best wine pairings.
DURATION 2 hours
TASTING 3 wines
PRICE €€

Picnic in the Garden
Families, friends, and couples are invited to take a tour of the estate followed by a country picnic served in a timeless, bucolic setting, with a warm, relaxed atmosphere.
DURATION 1½ hours
TASTING 3 wines
PRICE €€€

"La Bulle Verte" Bicycle Tour: All About Margaux
Château Prieuré-Lichine is the first in the Médoc region to have introduced these electric bicycle tours with itineraries available on a digital application. Follow the app and discover the secrets of the Margaux appellation through original content revealed at each stage of this beautiful route.
DURATION from 2 hours
PRICE €€€

20

CHÂTEAU D'ISSAN

TROISIÈME GRAND CRU CLASSÉ, MARGAUX

Authentic Margaux

Welcome to one of the oldest and most prestigious winemaking estates in the region. The fairy-tale château that awaits you at the end of a long drive through the vineyard dates from the seventeenth century, but Château d'Issan's reputation is much older: it was among the wines served at the twelfth-century wedding celebration of Eleonor of Aquitaine and the future king of England, Henry II. This reputation has withstood the test of time. Thomas Jefferson, when Ambassador to France, included Issan among his favorite Bordeaux vineyards.

GETTING THERE

Château d'Issan is located in Cantenac, fifteen miles (25 km) north of Bordeaux, or about a forty-minute drive away.

ADDRESS

Château d'Issan
Chemin de la Ménagerie
33 460 Margaux-Cantenac

CONTACT

+33 (0)5 57 88 35 91
château-issan.com

VINEYARD

Located in the heart of the Margaux appellation, Château d'Issan's vineyard spans 130 acres (53 ha) of gravel slopes and alluvial hills smoothed by erosion. Fifty-five percent of the parcels are planted with Cabernet Sauvignon, 40 percent with Merlot, 2 percent with Petit Verdot, 2 percent with Cabernet Franc, and 1 percent with Malbec.

MOTTO

In the late nineteenth century, Austria's emperor, Franz Joseph, coined the château's motto, engraved in stone above the door: *regvm mensis arisqve deorvm* ("for the table of kings and the altar of gods"). The current owners uphold this lofty ambition, while taking care not to intimidate amateurs, who are invited to come and learn about the work that goes in to creating such quality wines.

130 ACRES

(53 ha) of vines

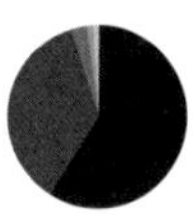

55% Cabernet Sauvignon
40% Merlot
2% Petit Verdot
2% Cabernet Franc
1% Malbec

SIGNATURE

Here, the vineyard is pruned each winter following Médoc tradition. Spring is a time for ploughing, desuckering, and debudding, followed in summer by a green harvest and leaf removal. In the fall, the château takes on about a hundred workers for the harvest, the culmination of a year's work. *Élevage* also follows Médoc tradition: the wines spend sixteen to eighteen months in French oak barrels, and every three months, the wine is racked and a candle is used to assess color and limpidity.

In 1945, the château was acquired, restored, and modernized by the Cruses, a family of Danish wine merchants. Today, the third generation, represented by Emmanuel Cruse and his brother and sister, own the château in partnership with Françoise and Jacky Lorenzetti, who own three other châteaux in the region.

TOURS & TASTINGS

La Tradition
Cross the moat to discover eight centuries of history in the château during this private tour, which culminates with a tasting of the grand cru and second wine.
DURATION 1½ hours
TASTING 2 wines
PRICE €€

La Mystérieuse
Following a private tour of the estate, you will have the opportunity to test your wine-tasting ability and try to identify three of the estate's wines in a blind tasting.
DURATION 1½ hours
TASTING 3 wines
PRICE €€

La Verticale
After a tour of the estate, the most discerning wine enthusiasts will have the honor of tasting three successive vintages in the private lounge.
DURATION 2 hours
TASTING 3 wines
PRICE €€€

La Royale
During this unique tasting experience, you'll savor four legendary vintages of this grand cru: 1995, 2005, 2010, and 2015.
DURATION 2 hours
TASTING 4 wines
PRICE €€€€

La Familiale
If you would like to end your visit by tasting the château's entire range of wines, then this is the tour for you.
DURATION 1½ hours
PRICE €€

Bicycle Tour in the Heart of the Domaine
Explore the vineyard by bicycle and discover the estate's many historical treasures. The tour includes a visit to the winery and barrel cellars, and ends on a high note with a tasting.

13

CHÂTEAU BRANE-CANTENAC

DEUXIÈME GRAND CRU CLASSÉ, MARGAUX

A historic terroir

"Be it a weakness or a strength, I have faith in my name, and I wish to gradually rechristen Gorse, to place it under the patronage of Brane-Cantenac," declared Baron de Brane in 1838, when he announced that his estate would have a new name and revealed the extent of his ambitions. His bold move would be no cause for embarrassment: Brane-Cantenac was classified a deuxième grand cru classé in the Margaux appellation fewer than twenty years later.

GETTING THERE

Château Brane-Cantenac is located about nineteen miles (30 km) from Bordeaux, or a forty-minute drive on the Bordeaux Wine Route (D2 highway), via Blanquefort, in Bordeaux's northern suburbs.

ADDRESS

Château Brane-Cantenac
Chemin de Benqueyre
33 460 Margaux-Cantenac

CONTACT

+33 (0)5 57 88 83 33
brane-cantenac.com

BRANE CANTENAC

SIGNATURE

The château was purchased by the Lurton family in 1925. Four generations later, Henri Lurton is at the helm. A winegrower at heart, Lurton grew up and still lives on the property. His philosophy is based on respect for the grapes and developing the terroir: he meticulously studies depth to the water table, as well as the composition and evolution of the soil in each parcel in order to determine the best varietals to plant.

Lurton has spent the last nearly thirty years equipping the estate with innovative technology. In 1999, an environmentally friendly, entirely revolutionary building was constructed to house the fermenting room and cellar. Featuring a large shuttered gallery and thermal regulation based on geothermal wells, the project is a powerful symbol of the estate's commitment to reducing its ecological footprint. Brane-Cantenac received Level 3 High Environmental Value certification from the French Ministry of Agriculture in 2019, which speaks to the château's efforts to support biodiversity and to use environmentally friendly plant protection agents, as well as to its excellent management of fertilization and water. For the last fifteen years, Brane-Cantenac has turned to the most qualified specialists in an effort to apply organic and biodynamic techniques, so that work on the estate continues to be more respectful of the environment. The finesse and elegance of the wines clearly reflect this search for the perfect balance.

VINEYARD

This 185-acre (75-ha) vineyard is one of the largest in the region. It includes an uninterrupted set of parcels covering more than seventy-four acres (30 ha) on the gravel and clay terrace in the northern part of the estate, on the Brane plateau. It also includes two islands of gravel and clay soil, and sand and gravel soil with large stones. The vineyard is planted primarily with Cabernet Sauvignon, as well as Merlot, Cabernet Franc, Petit Verdot, and Carmenère.

TOURS & TASTINGS

Discovery Tour
During this private, hour-long tour you will learn about the grape's journey from vine to bottle, as well as the essential steps needed in order to produce a great wine according to Henri Lurton's philosophy.
DURATION 1 hour
PRICE €€€

185 ACRES
(75 ha) of vines

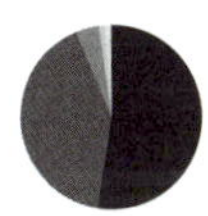

55% Cabernet Sauvignon
40% Merlot
3% Cabernet Franc
1% Petit Verdot
1% Carmenère

26

CHÂTEAU CANTENAC BROWN

TROISIÈME GRAND CRU CLASSÉ, MARGAUX

The soul of a great terroir
This imposing Tudor-style château was founded in 1806 and is named after the Scotsman John Lewis Brown, originally from Coulston, near Edinburgh. His grandson of the same name would become known for his naturalist engravings and paintings depicting battle scenes. A friend of Degas, Manet, Pissaro, and Toulouse-Lautrec, he made Cantenac Brown a place where artists and socialites gathered. The château is still infused with the aristocratic elegance of this storied past.

GETTING THERE

Château Cantenac Brown is located about nineteen miles (30 km) north of Bordeaux, or a forty-minute drive away.

ADDRESS

Château Cantenac Brown
Route d'Arsac
33 460 Margaux-Cantenac

CONTACT

+33 (0)5 57 88 81 81
cantenacbrown.com

155 ACRES
(63 ha) of vines

CHATEAU CANTENAC BROWN
CB
MARGAUX

SIGNATURE

Cantenac Brown has belonged to the Le Lous family since 2019. Tristan Le Lous works with José Sanfins, director of the property, sharing his desire to find a balance between nature and cultivation, as well as to pass on the heritage associated with the estate's recent history. Their pursuit of excellence is coupled with a deep respect for the environment, which inspired them to take on an ambitious project: the construction of a new 16,400-square-foot (5,000-m²) cellar made of raw earth and untreated wood, built within an existing building. A remarkable technical feat designed by architect Philippe Madec, the cellar will provide sufficient thermal inertia to eliminate the need for air-conditioning, with three-foot-(1-m-) thick walls and an underground duct that will ensure the flow of naturally cool air in the buildings. The cellar will deliver optimal technical functionality to support wine quality, making Cantenac Brown a pioneer in environmental responsibility.

VINEYARD

The 220-acre (63-ha) vineyard is located, for the most part, on the Margaux and Cantenac plateaus, and is planted with 65 percent Cabernet Sauvignon, 30 percent Merlot, and 5 percent Cabernet Franc. The variety of terroirs makes for a wealth of possibilities during blending.

TOURS & TASTINGS

Classic Tour
Château Cantenac Brown invites you to explore its grounds, which are steeped in its Scottish ancestry, as well as its arboretum and vineyards. Once you have familiarized yourself with the château's philosophy—sublimating the grape in its purest form—you will taste the grand cru and second red wine, BriO de Cantenac Brown.
DURATION 1 hour
TASTING 2 wines
PRICE €€

Vertical Tour
This vertical tasting of three grand cru vintages is preceded by a guided visit of the estate. Discover its terroir and unique history, as well as the secrets of vinification and barrel aging. And to top it all, after the tasting of three vintages, you will be presented with a mystery wine and challenged to identify it.
DURATION 1¼ hours
TASTING 4 wines
PRICE €€€

Masterclass
This masterclass includes a tour and a tasting, during which you will discover the importance of different types of glasses and how they affect your appreciation of the wine through the senses of sight, smell, and taste.
DURATION 1½ hours
TASTING 3 wines
PRICE €€€

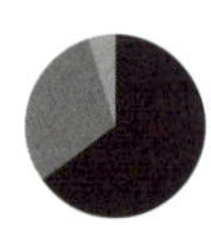

65% Cabernet Sauvignon
30% Merlot
5% Cabernet Franc

GRAND CRU CLASSÉ 1855
CHÂTEAU
CANTENAC BROWN
2010
MARGAUX

42

CHÂTEAU MARQUIS DE TERME

QUATRIÈME GRAND CRU CLASSÉ, MARGAUX

A distinguished free spirit
Founded in 1762, this château, located in the village of Margaux, is among the youngest grands crus classés in the 1855 classification. Despite its youth, Thomas Jefferson listed it in the third category of his selection of seventeen of the region's best wines, which he established in 1787. The Sénéclauze family has run the estate since 1935. Today, the château is known for its high-caliber wines, spiced with a dash of impertinence.

GETTING THERE

Château Marquis de Terme is located in the commune of Margaux-Cantenac, about nineteen miles (30 km) north of Bordeaux, or a forty-minute drive away. It is a seven-minute walk from Margaux train station.

ADDRESS

Château Marquis de Terme
3 Route de Rauzan
33 460 Margaux-Cantenac

CONTACT

+33 (0)5 57 88 86 43
château-marquis-de-terme.com

CHATEAU
QUIS DE TERME
DE BORDEAUX
2008

SIGNATURE

To cultivate its audacious identity while remaining true to the Margaux appellation, the estate relies on the remarkable discernment of its general manager, Ludovic David. For over ten years, this trained oenologist has analyzed the appellation and identified opportunities for innovation regarding soil composition, environmentally friendly strategies to fight diseases and parasites, and ecological management, as well as modernizing the cellars and vinification facilities. This approach has had a positive environmental impact and earned the estate High Environmental Value and ISO 14001 certifications.

Just like the young Théodore Sénéclauze, who, from 1890, had put into practice the radical idea of selling barreled wine by correspondence, the estate has no qualms about flouting the codes of Bordeaux grands crus classés: it was one of the first in this prestigious extended family to incorporate online sales. And finally, it should be noted that the team is mostly comprised of women—a rare phenomenon in the wine world for a château of this stature.

VINEYARD

The vineyard covers ninety-nine acres (40 ha) and is planted with three grape varieties: Cabernet Sauvignon (60 percent), Merlot (33 percent), and Petit Verdot (7 percent). The thick gravelly soil composed of quartz and quartzites, typical of Margaux, is reserved for Cabernet Sauvignon, except in areas where deep veins of clay are present, creating a more hospitable terroir for Merlot.

TOURS & TASTINGS

Château Marquis de Terme welcomes visitors seven days a week, with or without a reservation.

Zero CO_2 Day
Walk to the château from Margaux train station, then explore the vineyard by bicycle and bask in the fresh air. Gourmet nibbles will be waiting upon your return, served on the grounds with a glass of the château's grand cru.

WORKSHOPS

Grands Crus Classés 1855
Learn more about this historic wine classification and deepen your knowledge while strolling leisurely through the estate. This workshop includes tastings of five grands crus classés from the Médoc appellation, followed by a grand cru classé from the Barsac appellation and another from Sauternes. After this workshop, you will be an expert in grands crus classés from the left bank.
TASTING 7 wines
PRICE €€

FOOD & DRINK

Au Marquis de Terme
Château Marquis de Terme and chef Grégory Coutanceau have opened the very first restaurant in the heart of a Margaux estate, where the worlds of wine, French gastronomy, and hospitality converge—a concentration of French *art de vivre!*
PRICE €€€

Brunch
With two options, for adults or children, this wonderful opportunity to enjoy a gourmet meal in an idyllic setting is perfect for families, groups of friends, and couples.
PRICE €€

The Marquis's Tea Time
An unmissable chance to discover the universe of Château Marquis de Terme in a relaxed and welcoming atmosphere over a glass of wine, accompanied by the château's honey and jam served with bread, fresh fruit, and cookies.
PRICE €€

32

CHÂTEAU MARQUIS D'ALESME BECKER

TROISIÈME GRAND CRU CLASSÉ, MARGAUX

A world in its own right
The village of Margaux is home to a wine that has given rise to a world of its own. The fruit of exceptional terroir, centuries-old tradition, and modern creativity, Marquis d'Alesme is not only a fine wine, but also a singular vision of contemporary luxury, and embodies an elegant approach to reinventing a true art of living. In the eighteenth century, the Marquis d'Alesme, led by his taste for the exotic and the cosmopolitan, created his estate in Bordeaux. Here, culture thrived, characterized by a love of beauty and botany.

GETTING THERE

Château Marquis d'Alesme is located in the heart of Margaux, across from the city hall, about nineteen miles (30 km) north of Bordeaux, or a forty-minute drive away.

ADDRESS

Château Marquis d'Alesme Becker
7 Rue de la Trémoille
33 460 Margaux-Cantenac
CONTACT
+33 (0)5 57 81 13 20
contact@marquis.wine.com
marquisdalesme.wine.com

PHILOSOPHY

The Perrodo family now owns the estate, where this characterful wine brings together East and West. The château's architecture is a blend of French classicism and Asian symbolism: columns and arcades stand in perfect harmony alongside dragon scales and moon gates, while a sea of vines seems to stretch out to the horizon. Each detail reflects superlative sophistication and invites the visitor to indulge in a rare, poetic experience. A dreamlike utopia emerges against a backdrop of landscaped gardens, featuring delicate mosaics of colors and scents, sensory discoveries, and a magical interlude.

Embodying the philosophy that a great wine is a work of inspiration, Marquis d'Alesme offers an exceptional setting where the pleasures of the senses include aesthetic enjoyment and where visitors are invited to explore this unique world.

VINEYARD

The Marquis d'Alesme vineyard covers thirty-seven acres (15 ha). The Cabernet "family" reigns supreme here, making up 70 percent of the grape varieties used (63 percent Cabernet Sauvignon, 5 percent Petit Verdot, and 2 percent Cabernet Franc); Merlot represents the other 30%.

Elegant and refined, and often with a bouquet featuring floral and dark fruit aromas, Marquis d'Alesme wines are rich in flavor, with juicy notes of black current, blackberry, and blueberry, alongside well-balanced minerality.

FOOD & DRINK

Le Café des Simples
Tucked away in the Cour des Simples, in the estate's bucolic hamlet, the Café des Simples offers visitors a bite to eat and a place to relax. Platters of carefully chosen produce from local partners or the château's vegetable garden are available all day.
PRICE €€€

TOURS & TASTINGS

The Magical Interlude (private tour)
Prepare to have your senses enthralled and astonished by heady fragrances during this made-to-measure private visit. Embarking on a voyage of discovery, you will begin with a walk through Château Marquis d'Alesme's gardens, vineyard, fermenting room, and cellars. After exploring the château's natural surroundings and cultural influences, you will be transported by the exceptional workshop *Contes parfumés* (Fragrant Tales), after which you will taste two vintages of the cru classé, in the company of a wine specialist. The Magical Interlude continues in a dining room in the garden of the Cour des Simples, where you may continue the tasting experience in private.
DURATION 1½–2 hours
TASTING 2+ wines
PRICE €€€€

The Petit Marquis
This rare experience is offered free of charge and by appointment only. The Petit Marquis sweeps children aged from six to twelve into an imaginary world of wonder. A fairy-tale treasure hunt immerses little adventurers in the history of the château as they explore the estate in search of magical objects. They will journey into a world where everything is designed to spark their curiosity and awaken their senses.
PRICE Free of charge (by appointment only)

12

CHÂTEAU LASCOMBES

DEUXIÈME GRAND CRU CLASSÉ, MARGAUX

In praise of Merlot

Welcome to one of the largest vineyards in the region, producing a grand cru classé whose reputation has only improved with each new vintage. Over the centuries, ten generations of owners have succeeded the oldest known proprietor, Chevalier Antoine de Lascombes, including notable figures like the high priest of wine himself, Alexis Lichine—legendary oenologist and former confidant to Eisenhower and Churchill, who acquired the château in 1952 to ensure its success in the United States.

GETTING THERE

Château Lascombes is located about nineteen miles (30 km) north of Bordeaux, or a forty-minute drive away.

ADDRESS

Château Lascombes
1 Cours de Verdun
33 460 Margaux-Cantenac

CONTACT

+33 (0)5 57 88 70 66
château-lascombes.com

SIGNATURE

After periods of strife and of success resulting from the vagaries of history and nature, a US investment firm acquired the estate in 2001. Considerable investments were made and management entrusted to Dominique Befve, formerly of Lafite-Rothschild, who enlisted the help of the inimitable oenologist Michel Rolland. The MACSF, a French insurance company, kept the same team when it purchased the château in 2011.

Château Lascombes is unique in that it uses a significant amount of Merlot in its blend, resulting in a pleasingly smooth and supple wine.

Elements of seventeenth- and nineteenth-century architecture mingle in this château covered with Virginia creeper, while the interior is decidedly contemporary: in the first-year cellar, the lighting's blue halo showcases the purity of the traditional materials used.

VINEYARD

With 296 acres (120 ha) of vineyard located in the Margaux appellation and 28 acres (10 ha) in the Haut-Médoc appellation, the Lascombes terroir presents a wonderfully diverse soil profile, including a gravelly outcrop planted with Cabernet Sauvignon and Petit Verdot, a clay and gravel portion planted with Merlot and Cabernet Sauvignon, and, of course, its clay and limestone plots where Merlot finds its most favorable expression. Merlot is, in fact, the predominant grape variety in the vineyard, which is rare among Margaux crus.

TOURS & TASTINGS

Standard Tour
This guided tour of the fermenting room and wine cellars includes a tasting of two wines: Château Lascombes and Chevalier de Lascombes.
TASTING 2 wines
PRICE €

Private Standard Tour
In addition to the fermenting room and wine cellars, you will visit Lascombes' private bottle cellar, before tasting two wines: Château Lascombes and Chevalier de Lascombes.
TASTING 2 wines
PRICE €

Gourmet Tour
After a guided tour, you will enjoy pairings of the château's wines with a selection of artisanal chocolates.
PRICE €€

Epicurean Tour
Following a private visit of the château's facilities, you will be introduced to the aromatic complexity of four Lascombes grand cru classé vintages in the comfort of the tasting room.
TASTING 4 wines
PRICE €€

FOOD & DRINK

Picnic on the Grounds
This option includes a complete picnic basket accompanied by one of the château's wines. A sheltered space is provided in case of rain. Book at least one week in advance.
PRICE €

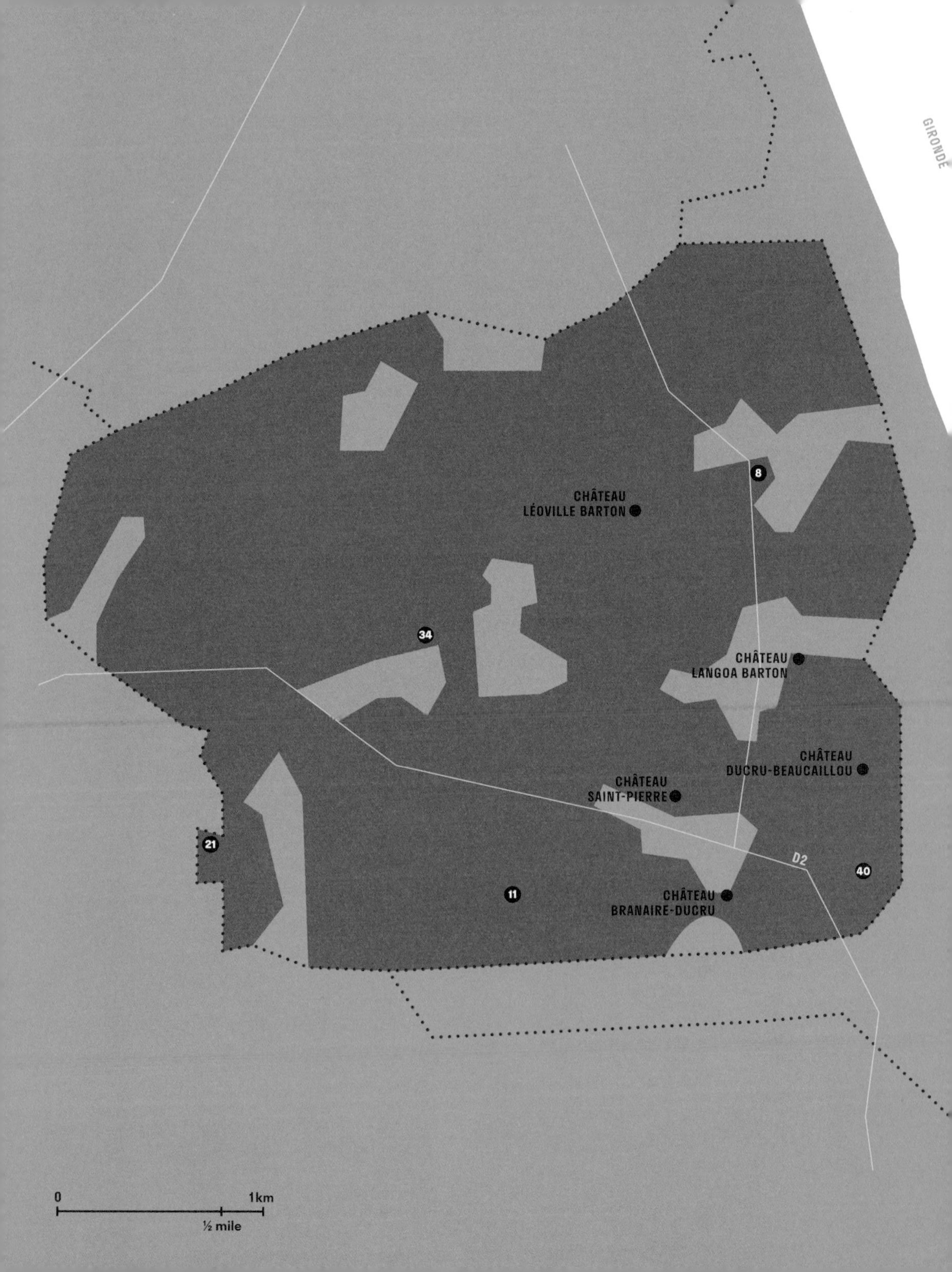
GIRONDE
8
CHÂTEAU LÉOVILLE BARTON
34
CHÂTEAU LANGOA BARTON
CHÂTEAU DUCRU-BEAUCAILLOU
CHÂTEAU SAINT-PIERRE
21
D2
40
11
CHÂTEAU BRANAIRE-DUCRU
0
1km
½ mile

MÉDOC

SAINT-JULIEN

- 40 Château Beychevelle
- 11 Château Gruaud Larose
- 21 Château Lagrange
- 34 Château Talbot
- 8 Château Léoville-Poyferré

40

CHÂTEAU BEYCHEVELLE

QUATRIÈME GRAND CRU CLASSÉ, SAINT-JULIEN

The Versailles of Bordeaux
Beychevelle is undeniably one of the most beautiful châteaux in the Bordeaux region. It is also one of the largest—its domain covers 618 acres (250 ha), of which 222 acres (90 ha) are planted with vineyards. The estate once even owned its own port on the Gironde estuary. It is said that the château derives its name from the Gascon *becha vela*, meaning "lower the sail," in reference to a tradition practiced by local sailors to indicate their allegiance to the Duke of Épernon, owner of the property and Grand Admiral of France in the seventeenth century.

GETTING THERE

Château Beychevelle is located at the entrance to Saint-Julien, about twenty-eight miles (45 km) north of Bordeaux, or an hour's drive on the Bordeaux Wine Route (D2 highway).

ADDRESS

Château Beychevelle
33 250 Saint-Julien-Beychevelle
CONTACT
+33 (0)5 56 73 20 70
beychevelle.com

618 ACRES
(250 ha) including
222 ACRES
(90 ha) of vines

56% Cabernet Sauvignon
40% Merlot
3% Petit Verdot
1% Cabernet Franc

HISTORY

Several exceptional women, including Marie-Amélie Kohn, Madame Guestier, Madame Heine, Marie-Louise Fould, and Élisabeth de Foucaud, have left their mark on the history and style of Beychevelle. Over the centuries, they contributed to a tradition of hospitality in which the beauty of the site was matched only by the gustatory quality of the grand cru. Beychevelle remains a favored haunt of artists, musicians, and authors, who regularly gather here for exhibitions, concerts, and other exclusive cultural events.

SIGNATURE

The château now belongs to Grands Millésimes de France, and the Castel and Suntory groups. In 2016, it was equipped with a new fermenting room and cellar designed by architect Arnaud Boulain. These facilities, which are more respectful of the fruit and of the environment, allow the château manager, Philippe Blanc, to express the full extent of his talent.
The new cellar is perfectly matched to the vineyard: each varietal has a place in the fermenting room, which is organized by parcel to bring out the complexity and depth of the estate's various terroirs.

VINEYARD

This 222-acre (90-ha) vineyard is planted with the varietals traditionally found in Médoc: 56 percent Cabernet Sauvignon, 40 percent Merlot, and several parcels of Cabernet Franc and Petit Verdot. The heart of the vineyard is located on the edge of the Gironde, on two plateaus of deep Garonne gravel from the Gunzian period, providing ideal conditions for Cabernet Sauvignon.

TOURS & TASTINGS

The Admiral's Tour
Navigate between tradition and modernity as you immerse yourself in three centuries of history in this former seigneury. Then discover the secrets of winegrowing and winemaking during a visit to the ultramodern cellar, before tasting the château's wine (options include two or three vintages).
DURATION 1¼ hours
TASTING 2–3 wines
PRICE €€€

The Secrets of the Winegrower
During this in-depth tour, you will discover the château's winery and cellars, and learn what it takes to make a high-quality wine. Your tour ends magnificently with a blind tasting of four vintages.
DURATION 1¾ hours
TASTING 4 wines
PRICE €€€

FOOD & DRINK/CHÂTEAU STAYS

La Table de Beychevelle
A far cry from the usual hotel accommodation on offer, the thirteen beautiful guest rooms and dining room at Château Beychevelle with their family house character offer the opportunity to sample local gastronomic dishes and to feel perfectly at home during your stay. In addition to serving lunch and dinner, La Table de Beychevelle is available for seminars and private functions, and even proposes customized helicopter tours of the vineyards of the Médoc and of the Bassin d'Arcachon.
PRICE €€€€

11

CHÂTEAU GRUAUD LAROSE

DEUXIÈME GRAND CRU CLASSÉ, SAINT-JULIEN

The wine of kings

The first vines were planted on these lands, which belonged to the Saint-Julien parish, by Chevalier Joseph Stanislas Gruaud. Legend has it, he erected the tower with the breathtaking view of the vineyards and the estuary in order to monitor growth, as well as to keep an eye on the workers. A French flag now flutters over its summit, but at that time, the château would have raised the flag of whichever country the wine was being made for in a given year: England, if the wine was fuller bodied and dark in color, Holland if it was lighter.

GETTING THERE

Slightly removed from the Bordeaux Wine Route (D2 highway), Gruaud Larose is located near the village of Beychevelle, about thirty miles (50 km) from Bordeaux, or a little more than an hour's drive away.

ADDRESS

Château Gruaud Larose
33 250 Saint-Julien-Beychevelle

CONTACT

+33 (0)5 56 73 89 43
gruaud-larose.com

202 ACRES
(82 ha) of vines

MOTTO

Near the end of the eighteenth century, the château was inherited by Joseph-Sébastien de Larose, an elected member of the provincial court of Bordeaux and lieutenant general of the seneschal of Guyenne. At the time, the vineyard was close to its current size. Appreciated by the nobility, Gruaud Larose grew in renown, and word of its reputation spread to the United States, where it was exported from that time on, propelled by a compelling motto: "Wine of kings, king of wines."

SIGNATURE

The château now belongs to the Merlaut family, who have undertaken a vast project of vineyard removal and replanting guided by a very long-term vision of optimizing the relationship between terroir and individual varietals to practice a more precise winegrowing method. The resulting elixir is renowned for its intense tannins and spicy notes, and a particularly memorable finish.

VINEYARD

The château's uniquely positioned, uninterrupted 202 acres (82 ha) form an island in the center of the Saint-Julien appellation. This largely homogenous vineyard features two main terroir profiles: hilltops of Gunzian gravel encourage the slow maturation that brings out the best in Cabernet Sauvignon, and clay and sandy soils that are rich in iron are perfectly suited to Merlot.

TOURS & TASTINGS

Essential Tour

If you only have an hour to spend at the château, don't miss this opportunity to climb the steps of the tower and take in the unparalleled view. A tour of the winemaking facilities is followed by a tasting of two wines. You may choose to expand this tasting with a food and wine pairing experience that includes a selection of traditional cheeses (mostly raw milk) or chocolates from an artisan chocolatier-confectioner in Saint-Laurent-Médoc, whose chocolate made with roasted chocolate nibs beautifully enhances the grand cru's intense, spicy notes.

DURATION 1 hour
TASTING 2 wines
PRICE €€€

Secrets of the Terroir

Wine enthusiasts will love this longer tour. After a walk through the vineyard, the visit continues on to the winemaking facilities and ends in the boutique, with a tasting of two of the château's wines and its honey. Tasting options are also offered (see Essential Tour).

DURATION 2½ hours
TASTING 2 wines
PRICE €€€€

Wine of Kings, King of Wines

This exceptional visit includes a complete tour of the vineyard, followed by a tasting of four vintages in the château's private rooms. Choose one of four different combinations of four different vintages.

DURATION 2 hours
TASTING 4 wines
PRICE €€€€

WORKSHOPS

Harvest Workshop

This half-day workshop—a celebration of the Médoc winemaking tradition—begins at 10:30 a.m. with an in-depth visit of the winemaking facilities and vineyard, where you'll taste different grape varieties straight from the vine. Then you'll tour the cellars, where the must and single-varietals will help you deepen your knowledge of wine. To top things off, the morning ends with an unforgettable lunch in the company of the grape pickers.

DURATION 4 hours
TASTING 2 wines
PRICE €€€€

Tasting and Cooking Classes

These two classes are ideal for those who wish to take their exploration of this grand cru classé and the local cuisine further.

DURATION 2 hours
TASTING 2 wines
PRICE €€€€

21

CHÂTEAU LAGRANGE

TROISIÈME GRAND CRU CLASSÉ, SAINT-JULIEN

An uncompromising quest for excellence

With 291 acres (118 ha) of vineyards that include the highest point in the Saint-Julien appellation, Château Lagrange is one of the largest estates in the region. It dates back to the seventeenth century—the first Lagrange domain is from 1630—and owes its troisième grand cru classé status in part to the innovations of Count Duchâtel, minister of the interior under Louis-Philippe and a pioneer in the area of vineyard drainage systems.

GETTING THERE

Château Lagrange is located thirty-one miles (50 km) north of Bordeaux, or a forty-minute drive away.

ADDRESS

Château Lagrange
33 250 Saint-Julien-Beychevelle

CONTACT

+33 (0)5 56 73 38 38
visites@chateau-lagrange.com
chateau-lagrange.com

INNOVATION

Today, the château directs its tradition of innovation toward environmental concerns. Acquired in 1983 by the Japanese Suntory group (the first non-Western group to acquire a grand cru in the region), for over twenty years Château Lagrange has been doing everything it can to support biodiversity in the vineyard: planting hedges, using sheep to mow its pastures and vineyards in mid-season, practicing late harvests, and planting wildflower meadows on fallow land. The first estate in Bordeaux to measure its carbon footprint, the château was also granted a "responsible farming" certification in 2005 and ISO 14001 certification in 2017, among others. In 2021, Lagrange was among the first thirteen companies to earn the "Bordeaux Cultivons Demain" (Let's Grow Bordeaux's Future) label: a collective project initiated by the Conseil Interprofessionnel du Vin de Bordeaux (Bordeaux Wine Council, CIVB) based on the principles of corporate social responsibility. The label reflects the château's commitments to the environment and society.

291 ACRES
(118 ha) of vines

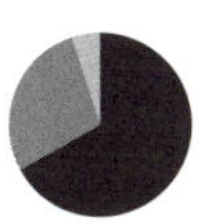

67% Cabernet Sauvignon
28% Merlot
5% Petit Verdot

TERROIR

Here, the terroir receives special care. The estate includes seventeen different types of soil and subsoil distributed across 103 plots, each with its own fermenting vat. Lagrange also maintains a practice of manual racking, using a candle to assess color and limpidity—a time-consuming and onerous method that requires great precision, but has the advantage of more closely respecting the identity of each wine.

VINEYARD

The Château Lagrange vineyard stretches over two Gunzian gravel slopes and spans 291 uninterrupted acres (118 ha). Ten of these are cultivated according to biodynamic guidelines and twenty according to organic principles, although they are not certified as such. The vineyard is planted with 67 percent Cabernet Sauvignon, 28 percent Merlot, and 5 percent Petit Verdot, distributed over more than one hundred individual plots, with vines averaging forty years old, and the oldest dating to 1952.

WINE TOURISM

The château offers visitors a wide range of experiences, from tastings and digital master classes to an opportunity to participate in the harvest and follow the grape's entire journey, from vine to vat. Lagrange even offers a fusion cuisine class led by on-site chef Taichi Sato, the highlight of the collaboration between the château's Japanese owner and its expert French teams. Guests will come to truly appreciate the precise aromatic profile of the château's wines through chef Sato's original pairings.

TOURS & TASTINGS/ WORKSHOPS

Tours

There are several different ways to discover the Château Lagrange vineyard and its wines, all culminating in a tasting of the château's four iconic wines.

TASTING 4 wines
PRICE €€€

Tastings for all levels

For a more nuanced tasting, sharpen your senses and put your palate to the test with the château's blending workshop, or try a blind, vertical tasting of four notable Lagrange vintages. Or visit the cellars for an immersive experience in the winemaker's world and be among the first to taste, directly from the barrel, the château's fine *en primeur* wine. The most enthusiastic oenophiles can even book an appointment with the château's oenologist for a tasting of older vintages.

Fusion Cuisine Class

Pull up a chair in the orangery and prepare yourself for a gastronomic experience that is unique in the region: a cooking class led by chef Taichi Sato. You'll learn to make two Japanese specialties using local, seasonal products, specially created to be paired with the estate's wines.

FOOD & DRINK/ CHÂTEAU STAYS

The château has fourteen guest rooms surrounded by vineyards and serves a "fusion lunch" in the former orangery, where guests are invited, in intimate groups, to enjoy wine and food pairings prepared by chef Taichi Sato. For groups of eight to twelve, a "wine and gastronomy" option, featuring a visit followed by lunch at the château, is also available.

34

CHÂTEAU TALBOT

QUATRIÈME GRAND CRU CLASSÉ, SAINT-JULIEN

An inherited love of wine

This centuries-old château is named for John Talbot, "Terror of the French": the most famous English general of the Hundred Years' War, who perished in the Battle of Castillon in 1453. The estate belonged to the Marquis d'Aux and his family for nearly two hundred years before being acquired by Désiré Cordier, who also owned the Meyney, Gruaud-Larose, and Lafaurie Peyraguey châteaux.

GETTING THERE

Château Talbot is located about thirty-one miles (50 km) north of Bordeaux, or about an hour's drive away.

ADDRESS

Château Talbot
33 250 Saint-Julien-Beychevelle

CONTACT

+33 (0)5 56 73 21 50
chateau-talbot.com

SIGNATURE

"In order to be a grand cru owner, you must in some way be in love with it," said Cordier, who described himself as a simple winegrower, yet was one of the most prominent twentieth-century figures in Bordeaux. His descendants inherited his love of wine, and today Nancy Bignon-Cordier, along with her husband, Jean-Paul, and their children, Philippine, Marguerite, and Gustave, continues to pursue the family tradition.

Château Talbot has a single cellar designed by Bordeaux architects Nairac and Vacheyrout. It features a coffered ceiling supported by a forest of concrete trees reminiscent of pruned grapevines. The aluminum glaze lining the walls bathes the cellar in soft light and gives added depth to the vast 4,900-square-foot (1,500-m²) space. No fewer than eighteen thousand casks of *grand vin* are lined up in the dimly lit cellar, which is maintained at a temperature of 63°F (17°C), to be aged for sixteen months.

The resulting wine is worthy of Désiré Cordier's aspirations of a century ago: Château Talbot wines are made for drinking young, but they can also be aged several decades in a good cellar. Silky tannins make them drinkable in the early years, before deepening and taking on aromatic complexity with age.

VINEYARD

The Talbot vineyard covers an impressive 272 acres (110 ha) in the Saint-Julien appellation. Located on the banks of the Gironde estuary, the vineyard is planted on hilltops of alluvial gravel swept along from the Massif Central by the Dordogne River and from the Pyrenees by the Garonne River. The vineyard is dominated by Cabernet Sauvignon, which occupies two-thirds of the surface area, compared with a little less than a third planted with Merlot, and a much smaller but crucial amount of Petit Verdot—Nancy Bignon-Cordier has a soft spot for this "enfant terrible."

TOURS & TASTINGS

Classic Tour
Discover the estate's long history and its sprawling vineyard, and visit its remarkable winemaking facilities, before tasting two red wines of the same vintage: Connétable Talbot and the château's grand cru classé.
DURATION 1 hour
TASTING 2 wines
PRICE €€

In the Gardens
In addition to visiting the vineyard and winemaking facilities, you will be invited to explore the château's private green spaces, including the grounds and a charming vegetable garden, before tasting two red wines of the same vintage: Connétable Talbot and Château Talbot.
DURATION 1½ hours
TASTING 2 wines
PRICE €€€

Prestige Tour
This option can be added to the Classic Tour and provides an overview of the château's twenty-first-century vintages. You will taste three exceptional vintages of the château's *grand vin*, as well as its white wine, Caillou Blanc.
DURATION 1½ hours
TASTING 3 wines
PRICE €€€€

272 ACRES
(110 ha) of vines

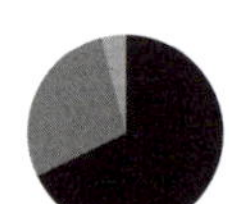

68% Cabernet Sauvignon
28% Merlot
4 % Petit Verdot

8

CHÂTEAU LÉOVILLE POYFERRÉ

DEUXIÈME GRAND CRU CLASSÉ, SAINT-JULIEN

Welcoming wines

The Léoville vineyard dates back to 1638, and was for many years the largest vineyard in the Médoc region. Château Léoville Poyferré was established on a portion of this land following a property division in 1840, and for the last century, it has belonged to the Cuvelier family, originally from the Lille region. In the 1980s, Didier Cuvelier breathed new life into the château by investing considerably to develop the vineyard and modernize the winemaking and cellar equipment. Management of the property was passed on to his cousin, Sara Lecompte Cuvelier, in 2018.

GETTING THERE

Château Léoville Poyferré is located about twenty-five miles (40 km) north of Bordeaux, on the outskirts of Pauillac, or a forty-minute drive away.

ADDRESS

Château Léoville Poyferré
38 Rue de Saint-Julien
33 250 Saint-Julien-Beychevelle

CONTACT

+33 (0)5 56 59 08 30
leoville-poyferre.fr

198 ACRES
(80 ha) of vines

31
32

LÉOVILLE
POYFERRÉ
LÉOVILLE
POYFERRÉ
LÉOVILLE
POYFERRÉ
LÉOVILLE
POYFERRÉ
LÉOVILLE
POYFERRÉ
LÉOVILLE
POYFERRÉ

SIGNATURE

The château emphasizes innovation in the fermenting room and tradition in the wine cellar. Cold maceration is carried out prior to fermentation to coax fruit aromas from the grapes and preserve their qualities; then the wine is transferred to oak barrels and aged for eighteen months. During aging, it is racked several times using a traditional, manual process and undergoes egg-white fining, a technique used since the sixteenth century to clarify red wines and soften their tannins. The house blend is of classic proportions, built on a generous foundation of Cabernet Sauvignon, with a considerable amount of Merlot assuring roundness and suppleness, and small but decisive additions of Cabernet Franc for delicacy and Petit Verdot providing tannins, freshness, and a hint of spice.

Nature is important to the teams at Léoville Poyferré, who choose to use organic enriching agents to maintain the soil's microbial balance and practice Guyot pruning: a gentle vine-training method that respects the natural flow of the vine's sap. The château has also implemented practices respectful of biodiversity, including "sexual confusion": a technique that involves releasing pheromones to combat vineyard pests, without resorting to insecticides.

VINEYARD

In the Médoc region, it is often said that the best land overlooks the river. With its view of the estuary, the Léoville Poyferré vineyard is no exception. Spanning 198 acres (80 ha), terraces of Mindel gravel contribute to producing consistent wines recognizable for their intense delicacy and elegance, enhanced by the warm temperatures of the estuary's microclimate.

WINE TOURISM

Visitors are met with a welcome befitting the owners' roots in northern France, and will hardly need persuading to enjoy the various on-site tasting and food and wine pairing experiences, all offered in a spirit of pleasure and generosity.

TOURS & TASTINGS

Tours of the château's winemaking facilities are followed by a seated, commented tasting.
DURATION 1 hour
PRICE €€

Here is a selection of specific tastings, among the many on offer.

Éclairée
This indulgent tasting pairs several vintages with chocolate, showcasing the creations of Hasnaâ: a young, talented artisan chocolatier based in Bordeaux.
DURATION 1¼ hours
PRICE €€€

Symphonie
This tasting unfolds with three fine vintages—2008, 2009, and 2010—accompanied by a selection of artisan charcuterie and cheese, all chosen for their delicacy, character, and ability to showcase the unique identity of Léoville Poyferré wines.
DURATION 1½ hours
PRICE €€€€

Impromptu Tastings
For travelers short on time, the boutique offers walk-in tastings, with no reservation required.

GIRONDE
D2
CHÂTEAU
BELGRAVE
38
56
CHÂTEAU
CANTEMERLE
CHÂTEAU
LA LAGUNE
0
5 km
3 miles

MÉDOC

HAUT-MÉDOC

56 Château de Camensac
38 Château La Tour Carnet

56

CHÂTEAU DE CAMENSAC

CINQUIÈME GRAND CRU CLASSÉ, HAUT-MÉDOC

Innovation steeped in tradition

This historic property appeared on the first detailed map of the French kingdom, drawn by the Cassini family for King Louis XIV. Its name is Gascon for "the path that leads to water." Several parasol pines tower over its buildings, most likely planted to alert Protestants fleeing persecution after the revocation of the Edict of Nantes that they could find refuge here.

GETTING THERE

Château de Camensac is located southwest of Saint-Laurent-Médoc, about thirty miles (48 km) north of Bordeaux, or an hour's drive away. Turn off the Bordeaux Wine Route (D2 highway) between Margaux and Pauillac at Beychevelle. The road to the château winds past its illustrious neighbors, the Gruaud-Larose and Lagrange châteaux.

ADDRESS

Château de Camensac
Route de Saint-Julien
33 112 Saint-Laurent-du-Médoc

CONTACT

+33 (0)5 56 59 41 69
chateaucamensac.com

FOOD & DRINK/ CHÂTEAU STAYS

Staying at Château La Tour Carnet is to embark on an incredible journey through time. Bernard Magrez restored the château's authentic medieval heritage in two incredible suites: the "Michel de Montaigne" and "La Boétie." The majestic dining room and elegant music room play host to one-of-a-kind experiences. From tastings of the château's exceptional vintages, to breakfasts fit for a king, to gastronomic meals with wine pairings, a myriad of timeless discoveries awaits guests at La Tour Carnet.

GUEST ROOMS 2 suites
TASTING gastronomic meals with wine pairings
PRICE €€€€

TOURS & TASTINGS

Tasting Tour

This comprehensive tour takes you into the medieval château, fermenting room, and barrel cellar for an in-depth explanation of the techniques used to create this grand cru classé—which is, of course, one of three wines offered in a tasting following the visit.

DURATION 1½ hours
TASTING 3 wines
PRICE €€

From Research to Innovation

During this award-winning tour, you'll have the unique opportunity to visit the plot where the château cultivates seventy-five different grape varieties in an effort to anticipate the effects of climate change and answer the key question of which varieties will define Bordeaux's future great wines. The tour includes a presentation of vinification and barrel-aging techniques, followed by a blind tasting of an impressive line-up of six single-varietal wines from Bernard Magrez's vineyards.

DURATION 2 hours
TASTING 6 wines
PRICE €€€

Gourmet Stroll

Extend your visit with a picnic in the château's gardens, before or after a tour and commented tasting of three wines, including the red Château La Tour Carnet.

DURATION 3 hours
TASTING 3 wines
PRICE €€€

Le Quatuor

Designed for the most demanding wine enthusiasts, this private tour of the château is led by a sommelier with in-depth knowledge of the estate as well as the art of winemaking and its history. The tour ends with a high-level tasting of four grands crus owned by Bernard Magrez: Château La Tour Carnet, Château Fombrauge, Château Pape Clément, and Clos Haut-Peyraguey.

DURATION 2 hours
TASTING 4 wines
PRICE €€€€

WORKSHOPS

Food and Wine Pairing Workshop

Following a tour of the estate, participate in a workshop led by Mademoiselle Margaux where you will learn to appreciate harmonious pairings of the château's wines with cheese or chocolate.

DURATION 1½ hours
TASTING 3 wines
PRICE €€€

B-Winemaker Workshop

This workshop is all about blending: you'll carry out the steps necessary to create your own bottle, including a taste analysis of mono-varietals, personalized blending (up to seven possible combinations), bottling, and label design. In the final step, your friends can taste your creation to see if you have what it takes to be a great winemaker.

DURATION 2 hours
TASTING 7 different assemblages
PRICE €€€€

CHÂTEAU
LAFITE-ROTHSCHILD
CHÂTEAU
CLERC MILON
CHÂTEAU
MOUTON
ROTHSCHILD
CHÂTEAU
D'ARMAILHAC
CHÂTEAU
PONTET-CANET
54
GIRONDE
D2
CHÂTEAU
GRAND-PUY-
DUCASSE
CHÂTEAU
DUHART-MILON
CHÂTEAU
CROIZET-BAGES
48
CHÂTEAU
GRAND-PUY-
LACOSTE
CHÂTEAU
HAUT-BAGES
LIBÉRAL
CHÂTEAU
LATOUR
49
44
CHÂTEAU
PICHON BARON
CHÂTEAU
PICHON LONGUEVILLE
COMTESSE
DE LALANDE
CHÂTEAU
HAUT BATAILLEY
0
1km
½ mile

MÉDOC

PAULLAC

44

CHÂTEAU BATAILLEY

CINQUIÈME GRAND CRU CLASSÉ, PAUILLAC

A historical landmark
Located in the heart of the Pauillac appellation, Château Batailley is named for a battle that took place on its land near the end of the Hundred Years' War, in 1543, when Charles VII's troops put an end to the siege of Bordeaux. They recaptured the neighboring Château Latour, which had been occupied by Anglo-Gascon troops since 1378.

GETTING THERE

Château Batailley is located about thirty-one miles (50 km) north of Bordeaux, or an hour's drive away.

ADDRESS

Château Batailley
Route de Batailley
33 250 Pauillac
CONTACT
+33 (0)5 56 59 24 49
batailley.com

HISTORY

The property of the Borie family for nearly a century, the château now belongs to their descendants, the Castéja family, who also operate the wine merchant group Borie-Manoux. The château is steeped in history and is home to an imposing eighteenth-century residence with a garden designed by Barillet Deschamps—gardener to Napoleon III and Empress Eugénie—as well as an exhibition hall constructed by Gustave Eiffel for the 1889 World's Fair in Paris. It had to be disassembled for transport to the property, where today it regularly plays hosts to concerts and other events.

SIGNATURE

All of the parcels here are worked and are analyzed every three years in order to determine the soil profile of each one. Fertilization plans that will maintain healthy soil microbiomes are developed based on knowledge of naturally present minerals. Vinification takes place in a fermenting room equipped with fifty-eight vats, one for each parcel; the wines are aged in French barrels, in first-year cellars, then transferred to second-year cellars to be aged for another sixteen to eighteen months, before being bottled, unfiltered, at the château.

VINEYARD

Covering 148 acres (60 ha), the vineyard is located on the magnificent gravel plateau facing the château and is planted with classic grape varieties, including a clear majority of Cabernet Sauvignon, a quarter of Merlot, and more modest proportions of Cabernet Franc and Petit Verdot.

EVENTS

Château Batailley regularly hosts concerts during the Estivales en Musique du Médoc, the only music festival in Europe to exclusively program young laureates of international music competitions.
PRICE €

TOURS & TASTINGS

Tours of the château's cellars and gardens are available by appointment only.
PRICE €

148 ACRES
(60 ha) of vines

70% Cabernet Sauvignon
25% Merlot
3% Petit Verdot
2% Cabernet Franc

CHATEAU
BATAILLEY

49

CHÂTEAU LYNCH-MOUSSAS

CINQUIÈME GRAND CRU CLASSÉ, PAUILLAC

Time-honored distinction
Originally a hunting lodge, the château is located on beautiful tree-filled grounds, far removed from the busy city. Over the course of its four-hundred-year history, the estate has passed through the hands of three families: the Lynches, descendants of an Irish soldier who settled in Bordeaux; the Vasquez, a family of Spanish merchants; and the Castéjas, who own several other prestigious grand cru estates. Upon the death of Jean-Baptiste Lynch in 1835, part of the estate was split, giving rise to Château Lynch-Moussas. In the 1970s, after a long period of undivided coownership and subsequent decline, the château underwent a transformation. "We took our time—the time the vineyard needed," explains Philippe Castéja who, since the early 2000s, has played an instrumental role in returning the château to its former glory.

GETTING THERE

Château Lynch-Moussas is located about thirty-one miles (50 km) north of Bordeaux, or an hour's drive away, via the D1215.

ADDRESS

Château Lynch-Moussas
Route de Batailley
33 250 Pauillac

CONTACT
+33 (0)5 56 00 00 70
domaines@borie-manoux.fr
lynch-moussas.com

VINEYARD

The Château Lynch-Moussas vineyard covers 153 acres (62 ha) in the southwest region of the Pauillac appellation and borders the vineyards of Pauillac's other grands crus classés, such as Châteaux Latour, Lynch-Bages, Pichon-Longueville Baron, Grand-Puy-Lacoste, and Batailley. The vineyard features two soil types, one rich in fine gravel, planted with Cabernet Sauvignon (75 percent of the vineyard), and plots with veins of clay running through them, reserved for Merlot.

TOURS & TASTINGS

Tours of Château Lynch-Moussas's wine cellar and gardens are available to the public by appointment only.
PRICE €€

75% Cabernet Sauvignon
25 % Merlot

CHATEAU
LYNCH-MOUSSAS
2007

48

CHÂTEAU LYNCH-BAGES

CINQUIÈME GRAND CRU CLASSÉ, PAUILLAC

The Pauillac way of life

The name Lynch-Bages reflects the paradox inherent in a region rooted in its terroir but open to new horizons. Bages is actually the name of the hamlet of winemakers that was wonderfully restored by Jean-Michel Cazes, while Lynch is the name of a family of wine merchants descended from a native of Galway, who fled Ireland in the late seventeenth century.
The Cazes family has managed the château since 1939; Jean-Charles, then his son André would forge the identity of this cru classé. André's son Jean-Michel settled here in Pauillac in 1973, before passing the reins to Jean-Charles Cazes, who undertook renovations in the 2020s.

GETTING THERE

Château Lynch-Bages is located a few hundred yards south of the town of Pauillac, and thirty-six miles (58 km) from Bordeaux, or an hour's drive on the Bordeaux Wine Route (D2 highway).

ADDRESS

Château Lynch-Bages
Route de Batailley
33 250 Pauillac

CONTACT

+33 (0)5 56 73 19 31
visit@jmcazes.com
lynchbages.com

247 ACRES
(100 ha) of Garonne gravel

CHATEAU
LYNCH BAGES

ARCHITECTURE

Jean-Charles Cazes commissioned American architect Chien Chung Pei to equip Lynch-Bages with a vast, glass building—as elegant as it is functional—that houses the fermenting room, a large harvest reception area, and offices. A new underground cellar has the capacity to accommodate two harvests at once. There, the team can work without space limitations and optimize aging times for the wines. The 2020 vintage is the first to be vinified in the new facilities.

Through these efforts, Lynch-Bages focuses modernity, refinement, and respect for the environment into winemaking excellence. The château's *grand vin* is still made in the style created by the first Jean-Charles Cazes in the late 1930s: a combination of structure, finesse, and elegance that offers generous aromas in its youth and develops deeper complexities characteristic of Pauillac's *grands vins* with bottle age.

VINEYARD

The 247-acre (100-ha) vineyard located on the Bages plateau occupies several hilltops of Garonne gravel that make up the appellation's finest terroirs. Soil analysis was conducted using satellite cartography to identify the parcels best adapted to Cabernet Sauvignon, Petit Verdot, Merlot, and Cabernet Franc. In an effort to preserve genetic diversity in the vineyard, massal selection is used to identify and replant grafts from the hardiest rootstock.

FOOD & DRINK/CHÂTEAU STAYS

Café Lavinal
Adjoining the château, this restaurant created in 2006 is named after Jean-Michel Cazes's grandmother, Berthe Lavinal, who was a talented cook. It is an address worth noting for anyone who appreciates simple, seasonal cuisine enjoyed in the presence of winegrowers and locals.
PRICE €€€

Château Cordeillan-Bages
Five-star hotel
Château Cordeillan-Bages is a former *chartreuse* built in the style typical of the Médoc region. Since 1989, when it became a splendid Relais & Châteaux property, it has become an essential stop on the Bordeaux Wine Route (D2 highway).
PRICE €€€€

TOURS & TASTINGS

Visits are available to the public by appointment only, from Monday to Saturday.
PRICE €€

Village of Bages
This charming hamlet was completely renovated in the 2000s by Jean-Michel Cazes, who grew up there. His desire was to create a destination dedicated to the art of Médoc hospitality. In addition to Café Lavinal, you will find the Bages' Bazaar boutique, which offers a large selection of wines, tableware, and home décor. The Pignon butcher stocks high-quality meat and regional specialties. Atelier Vélo offers bicycles for rent, allowing you to explore the region's roads. Wine aficionados can also learn the secrets to the art of blending, with the company VINIV, and create their very own customized fine wine.

54

CHÂTEAU PÉDESCLAUX

CINQUIÈME GRAND CRU CLASSÉ, PAUILLAC

Pauillac's finest terroirs
This estate was created in the early nineteenth century by Pierre-Urbain Pédesclaux, a wine merchant operating out of Bordeaux's Quai des Chartrons. In 1855, when the château was classified as a grand cru, the vineyard covered less than twenty-five acres (10 ha). Counts François Xavier Marie Rolland de Chambaudoin d'Erceville and Michel Perrin du Lac, sons-in-law of Bernard de Lévezou de Vésins, took the reins in 1919. In 1930, management of the estate was entrusted to Lucien Jugla, who purchased the château twenty years later. In 2009, the Jugla family sold the property, including its sixty-nine-acre (28-ha) vineyard, to the Lorenzetti family, who had purchased Château Lilian Ladouys the previous year.

GETTING THERE

Château Pédesclaux is located north of Pauillac, about forty miles (64 km) from Bordeaux, or an hour-and-fifteen-minute drive, and is of equal distance from the Gironde estuary and Château Mouton-Rothschild.

ADDRESS

Château Pédesclaux
Route de Pédesclaux
33 250 Pauillac

CONTACT
+33 (0)5 56 59 22 59
contact@chateau-pedesclaux.com
chateau-pedesclaux.com

COMMITMENT

The vineyard was entirely restructured and its surface area progressively expanded to reach 118 acres (48 ha). The new cellars went into operation in 2014. Four years later, Manon Lorenzetti joined her parents in running the estate and is overseeing a gradual conversion to organic farming. Half of the vineyard is managed according to biodynamic principles, which earned the estate organic certification in 2022.

This commitment to organic agriculture allows for a full expression of Pauillac's excellent terroirs by taking advantage of the nineteen soil types found within the most prestigious areas of the appellation.

VINEYARD

The vineyard occupies 118 acres (48 ha) of deep gravel where clay and limestone may also be found, distributed throughout Pauillac's finest terroirs. Fifty-nine percent of the vineyard is planted with Cabernet Sauvignon, 32 percent with Merlot, 5 percent with Cabernet Franc, and 4 percent with Petit Verdot.

118 ACRES
(48 ha) of deep gravel

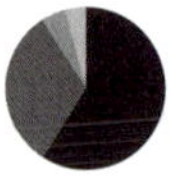

59% Cabernet Sauvignon
32% Merlot
5% Cabernet Franc
4% Petit Verdot

ARCHITECTURE

The architect Jean-Michel Wilmotte was tasked with renovating the château in 2012. He undertook construction of an entirely gravity-fed cellar designed to convey an aesthetic of elegance and transparency. Smooth glass and subtle scaffolding frame the pale stones of the building, polished by time, and the graceful curves of the dovecote.

TOURS & TASTINGS

Château Tour

Discover the history of the estate and the details of its architecture. This tour includes a visit to the fermenting room and cellar, followed by a tasting of two of the château's wines.
DURATION 2 hours
TASTING 2 wines
PRICE €
PRIVATE TOUR Possible to reserve as a private tour for up to eight people
PRICE (fixed) €€€€

Vertical Tasting

After a guided visit of the property, fermenting room, and barrel cellar, you will be treated to a tasting of five vintages of this cru classé.
DURATION 2 hours
TASTING 5 wines
PRICE (fixed) €€€€ for up to eight people

Chocolate and Wine Pairing

This experience includes a tour of the château, followed by a tasting of two wines paired with two chocolates specially selected by Bordeaux-based artisan chocolatier Hasnaâ.
DURATION 1½ hours
TASTING 2 wines
PRICE €

1997
1996
1998

GIRONDE
CHÂTEAU CALON SÉGUR
CHÂTEAU MONTROSE
CHÂTEAU COS LABORY
17
D2
39
0
1km
½ mile

MÉDOC

SAINT-ESTÈPHE

17

CHÂTEAU COS D'ESTOURNEL

DEUXIÈME GRAND CRU CLASSÉ, SAINT-ESTÈPHE

The Maharajah's 1001 terroirs

The sight of the striking pagodas of this château, perched on a steep slope in Saint-Estèphe, is enough to make even the most uninformed visitor realize they have happened upon an extraordinary place. The pioneering Louis Joseph Gaspard Lacoste de Maniban, Marquis of Estournel, inherited this gravelly mound in 1791. He devoted years and considerable financial resources to erecting the magnificent château, in addition to shaping a wine that reflects the richness and complexity of the surrounding terroir.

GETTING THERE

Château Cos d'Estournel is located about thirty-seven miles (60 km) north of Bordeaux, or an hour-and-a-half drive away. The château is also equipped with a heliport.

ADDRESS

Château Cos d'Estournel
Cos S
33 180 Saint-Estèphe

CONTACT

+33 (0)5 56 73 15 50
estournel.com

DISCOVERY

It is not uncommon to come across an admiring description of this château in French literature. Stendhal was enchanted by it, praising its elegance in his 1835 *Voyage dans le Midi de la France*. Saint-Amand expressed astonishment at the theatrical dimension of its "marvelous entrance," and was surprised to learn that the building housed only a cellar and stables at the time; the manor house was located behind it.

VINEYARD

The plots at Château Cos d'Estournel are spread over 247 acres (100 ha). The property features a particularly diverse combination of soil profiles and orientations that create myriad terroirs, each adding complexity to the wine. The central portion of the vineyard is located on a plateau of deep gravel with, on either side, hills facing east and south respectively. A vein of clay runs diagonally through the entire estate. Two-thirds of the vineyard is planted with Cabernet Sauvignon, complemented by Merlot and a small percentage of Cabernet Franc and Petit Verdot.

SIGNATURE

Since 2000, this deuxième cru has belonged to Michel Reybier, a worthy successor to his visionary forebear. In 2008, Reybier ordered the construction of the first winemaking facilities in Bordeaux to rely on gravity, rather than pumps, to transfer wine, from harvest to bottling. This gentler process helps keep the grapes intact as the fruit and juice is handled, so much so that each fruit is distinguishable after vinification, during crush. The following steps—fermentation, aging, and racking—also harness the power of gravity.

This attention to detail carries through to the vineyard, which is cared for with a meticulous respect for nature and the composition of each soil type present on the estate; groups of vines are identified by variety, age, orientation, and quality. This is winemaking elevated to art.

247 ACRES
(100 ha) of vines

TOURS & TASTINGS

Private Tour
Learn about the fascinating history of the "Maharajah of Saint-Estèphe," the vineyard's unmatched orientation, its diverse terroir, and its gravity-fed cellar housed beneath pagodas of Asian inspiration.

In the Footsteps of the Maharajah
This option includes a full tour of the winery and a tasting of six wines, including four Cos d'Estournel vintages.
DURATION 2–3 hours
TASTING 6 wines

Treasures of the Maharajah
This tour is identical to the previous one, except for the vintages. You will have the opportunity to taste wine from the exceptional years of 1982, 2005, 2009, and 2016.
DURATION 2–3 hours
TASTING 6 wines

FOOD & DRINK

Lunch at the Château
You can extend certain tours with an exceptional meal: opt for lunch at the château, in the company of a guide, and taste Cos d'Estournel wines paired with gastronomic dishes made from local produce. From Monday to Friday.

CHÂTEAU STAYS

Maison d'Estournel
Come and unwind a few hundred yards from the castle, facing the vineyards, in one of the fourteen rooms located in the former private residence of Louis Gaspard d'Estournel. Designer Alex Michaelis drew inspiration from the bucolic surroundings and selected fine, natural materials to recreate the spirit of a country home, as requested by Michel Reybier. This exceptional setting is quite unlike any conventional hotel.
WEBSITE lamaison-estournel.com

39

CHÂTEAU LAFON-ROCHET

QUATRIÈME GRAND CRU CLASSÉ, SAINT-ESTÈPHE

A handsome estate
Château Lafon-Rochet is nothing if not elegant. With its Tuscan-yellow *chartreuse* that was built in the 1960s but modeled after the eighteenth-century architecture typical of the region, a fermenting room lit up like a theater set, and a stunning wine cellar suffused with a unique tranquility, it is the epitome of refinement.

GETTING THERE

Château Lafon-Rochet is located near Château Cos d'Estournel and Château Lafite-Rothschild, about thirty-one miles (50 km) north of Bordeaux, or an hour's drive away.

ADDRESS

Château Lafon-Rochet
Blonquet Ouest
33 180 Saint-Estèphe

CONTACT

+33 (0)5 56 59 32 06
lafon-rochet.com

CHÂTEAU
LAFON-ROCHET
08
189hl
C8
Lafon-Rochet
2016

SIGNATURE

The estate dates back to the early eighteenth century, when Étienne de Lafon, a parliamentarian from the Gironde, planted the vineyard on his newly acquired property located in the hamlet of La Rochette in Saint Estèphe. After passing through the hands of four different owners, the château was purchased by the Tesseron family, who shaped its current identity over the years with determination and a touch of humor—Michel Tesseron would describe himself as a chef who could only produce one dish a year. "After years of considering ways to reduce our effect on the environment, we asked ourselves what we could do to make a positive impact," explains Basile Tesseron, who has applied agroforestry techniques to the entire vineyard. Over a two-year period, nearly five thousand vines were removed and six thousand trees planted to achieve a balance between the vineyard and the natural environment.

The property was recently acquired by the Lorenzetti family, who purchased the neighboring château, Lilian Ladouys, in 2008. They also own Pédesclaux, in Pauillac, and have a 50 percent share in Château d'Issan.

VINEYARD

The uninterrupted ninety-nine-acre (40-ha) estate bordering Pauillac overlooks Château Lafite-Rothschild. The vineyard is planted with 47 percent Cabernet Sauvignon, 45 percent Merlot, 4 percent Cabernet Franc, and 4 percent Petit Verdot, in gravelly soil on a clay and limestone bedrock at an altitude of between sixteen and eighty-two feet (5–25 m).

TOURS & TASTINGS

Tasting Only
Don't miss this opportunity to taste the château's grand cru and second wine, Les Pèlerins de Lafon-Rochet. You can choose to taste either one vintage of each wine, or two vintages of the grand cru and one vintage of the second wine.
TASTING 2–3 wines
PRICE €–€€

Tradition Tour
This guided tour of the winemaking facilities includes a tasting of the château's second wine and grand cru.
DURATION 1 hour
TASTING 2 wines
PRICE €

Experience Tour
This guided tour of the winemaking facilities includes a barrel tasting of the *en primeur* vintage, followed by a tasting of the second wine and two vintages of the grand cru.
DURATION 1½ hours
TASTING 3 wines
PRICE €

Vintage Tour
This tour is identical to the Experience Tour, but includes a vertical tasting of five wines.
DURATION 2 hours
TASTING 5 wines
PRICE €€

99 ACRES
(40 ha) of vines

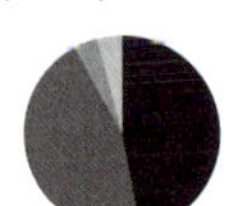

47% Cabernet Sauvignon
45% Merlot
4% Petit Verdot
4% Cabernet Franc

GRAND CRU CLASSÉ EN 1855
CHÂTEAU
LAFON-ROCHET

DORDOGNE
BORDEAUX
A630
GARONNE
5
0
5 km
3 miles

MÉDOC

PESSAC

5 Château Haut-Brion

5

CHÂTEAU HAUT-BRION

PREMIER GRAND CRU CLASSÉ, PESSAC

Le Pavillon Catelan
The Marquis de Catelan had this residence built in the early nineteenth century to make use of part of Château Haut-Brion at a time when the property was divided between two heirs. Over the decades, it was expanded, modified, and even housed the château's winegrowers, once the estate was reunited in 1841.

GETTING THERE

Château Haut-Brion and Le Pavillon Catelan are located less than 3 miles (5 km) from the center of Bordeaux, near the beltway and the A10 highway.

ADDRESS

Château Haut-Brion
135 Avenue Jean Jaurès
33 608 Pessac

CONTACT

+33 (0)5 56 00 29 30
haut-brion.com

ARCHITECTURE

The building was recently rehabilitated and enlarged to create different reception areas for the public with remarkably welcoming, refined interior design.

Since July 2021, the ground level has been home to one of the most beautiful wine boutiques in the region, the Cave du Château, Bordeaux. The impressive selection features numerous vintages of wines from the family-owned estates, including large formats, as well as more surprising bottles that are sure to delight informed wine enthusiasts.

TOURS & TASTINGS

Private tastings can be arranged by appointment only. An online catalog is available on the website lacaveduchateau.com.

DISCOVER THE FINE SWEET WHITE WINES

SAUTERNAIS

The Sauternais region encompasses strikingly different appellations cultivated in the deep gravel soils on the rolling hills of Sauternes and the red soils of Barsac's limestone plateau. Here, the cold waters of the Ciron River, which flows in the shade of the valley's thousand-year-old beech forest—itself an incredible haven of biodiversity—meet the warmer waters of the Garonne. Where they mingle, early morning mists appear, creating the perfect conditions for the development of *Botrytis cinerea*, a unique, microscopic fungus that gives rise to a wine with unrivaled complexity and richness.

CHÂTEAU NAIRAC
CHÂTEAU SUAU
GARONNE
CHÂTEAU BROUSTET
73
67
CHÂTEAU CAILLOU
CHÂTEAU DOISY-DUBROCA
74
68
CHÂTEAU DOISY-VÉDRINES
A62
CIRON
0
1km
½ mile

SAUTERNAIS

BARSAC

73 Château de Myrat
67 Château Coutet
74 Château Doisy Daëne
68 Château Climens

73

CHÂTEAU DE MYRAT

DEUXIÈME GRAND CRU CLASSÉ, BARSAC

A family affair

Located on the limestone plateau of Haut-Barsac, Château de Myrat was built in the eighteenth century by the Demirat family. Since 1937, it has belonged to the Pontac family, whose ancestors include Arnaud de Pontac: a prominent figure in Bordeaux winemaking, who, in the seventeenth century, used his Haut-Brion terroir to introduce the notion of linking a cru with a clearly delineated terroir. His idea soon spread throughout Europe. After a decade of inactivity, the estate underwent a renaissance in 1988, gradually being restored by the family to its former glory and its rightful place among Bordeaux's great wines. Two of the family's descendants, Slanie and Élisabeth, now manage the estate.

GETTING THERE

Château de Myrat is located about twenty-five miles (40 km) south of Bordeaux, or a forty-minute drive on the A62 highway.

ADDRESS

Château de Myrat
33 720 Barsac
CONTACT
+33 (0)5 56 27 09 06
chateaudemyrat.fr

74 ACRES
(30 ha) including

54 ACRES
(22 ha) of vines

ENDURING ENCHANTMENT

A visit to Château de Myrat is a timeless experience. The uninterrupted property is home to an elegant eighteenth-century *chartreuse* surrounded by fifty-four acres (22 ha) of vineyards and a magnificent twenty-acre (8-ha) park featuring century-old trees, an English garden, heritage species of fruit trees, and several aviaries, where peacocks, geese, pheasants, and other birds live peacefully.

VINEYARD

Planted on a terroir of limestone covered with a fine layer of clay, the vineyard, lined with low walls, is planted with 88 percent Sémillon, 8 percent Sauvignon, and 4 percent Muscadelle. Slanie and Élisabeth blend these varieties to create an elegant Sauternes with the fresh minerality typical of the terroir.

TOURS & TASTINGS

Discovery Tour
Visit the estate, including the vineyards and park, followed by the beautiful barrel cellar and collection of old-fashioned presses. Soak up the rich family history and find out more about how these magical wines are made here with biodiversity in mind. The visit ends on a high note with a tasting of three vintages of the grand cru (young, ten years, and twenty years).
DURATION 1 hour
TASTING 3 wines
PRICE €€

Perfect Pairing Tour
This option can be added to the Discovery Tour. Discover delicious pairings between Château de Myrat's wines and a selection of cheeses.
DURATION 1½ hours
TASTING 3 wines
PRICE €€

NOTE: Follow Château de Myrat on Facebook or Instagram to be informed of its unforgettable summer after-work events.

FOOD & DRINK

Picnic in the Park
In the mood for a pleasant, convivial experience? The château invites you to enjoy a locally sourced picnic served in its gardens, in the shade of century-old trees, and accompanied by a glass of Château de Myrat. Outdoor games are also available upon request.
PRICE €€€

Lunch in the Château Kitchen
Enjoy unique food and wine pairings around the château's fireplace. Reservations (for groups of at least six) should be made three days ahead.

67

CHÂTEAU COUTET

PREMIER GRAND CRU CLASSÉ, BARSAC

A nervy aristocrat

Dating back to the seventeenth century, this premier cru is one of the oldest vineyards in the appellation. Originally built as a British stronghold during the Hundred Years' War, the château stills bears the mark of its medieval origins in the thirteenth-century square tower at its center. After the French Revolution, the château belonged to the Lur-Saluces family, which produced Napoleon's chamberlain, and later to Henri-Louis Guy, an industrialist from Lyon and inventor of a vertical winemaking press. Since 1977, the Baly family, originally from Alsace, has owned the château, and management has been handed down the generations. Today, Philippe and his niece, Aline Baly, maintain this legendary estate.

GETTING THERE

Château Coutet is located about twenty-five miles (40 km) southeast of Bordeaux, or a forty-minute drive away.

ADDRESS

Château Coutet
33 720 Barsac

CONTACT

+33 (0)5 56 27 15 46
chateaucoutet.com

104 ACRES
(42 ha) of vines

CHATEA
COUT
1ER CRU CLASS

SIGNATURE

The château's terroir lies within a triangle formed by the ocean, the river, and the forest, with the Ciron flowing through it. Because the land is among the coldest in the appellation, the grapes mature more slowly than on neighboring Sauternes estates. An exceptional microclimate and limestone soils give these gold and opal wines a freshness and liveliness that are particularly appreciated in sweet white wines. The word *coutet* is derived from the Gascon word for "knife," and elegantly evokes the edgy nerviness characteristic of the château's style.

Harvesting takes place between September and November. Manual picking lasts between thirty and forty days, and includes several stages of hand-sorting that require great care and patience. After a slow, gentle press, the juices are transferred to French oak casks to age for eighteen months before assemblage, when experienced and new cellar masters combine their expertise to produce truly miraculous wines.

VINEYARD

The undivided vineyard spans 104 acres (42 ha) and, following tradition in this appellation, is planted with a majority of Sémillon, as well as a quarter of Sauvignon and a smaller proportion of Muscadelle. It is located thirty-nine feet (12 m) above sea level on a plateau of clay and sandy gravel resting on limestone bedrock.

TOURS & TASTINGS

Classic and Premium Tours
After a tour of the vineyard and winery, you will have the option of tasting two or three wines.
TASTING 2–3 wines
PRICE €€

Discover Sauternes and Barsac Varietals
This tour is followed by an introduction to the appellations' grape varieties in the form of grape jelly, accompanied by a tasting of two wines.
TASTING 2 wines
PRICE €€€

Blind Tasting
Take this challenge with your eyes closed! Following a tour of the estate, gather a group of at least four for a blind tasting of four vintages of this premier grand cru classé.
TASTING 4 wines
PRICE €€€

Evolution of Sweet Wines
Savor and compare three vintages of this premier grand cru classé from different decades, following a tour of the vineyard and winery.
TASTING 3 wines
PRICE €€€

FOOD & DRINK

Château Coutet offers private lunch and dinner options at the château, in the company of Aline or Philippe Baly, or, for larger groups, in the wine cellar.

CHÂTEAU 6–8 guests
CELLAR 9–35 guests

74

CHÂTEAU DOISY DAËNE

DEUXIÈME GRAND CRU CLASSÉ, BARSAC

GETTING THERE

Château Doisy Daëne is located about twenty-five miles (40 km) south of Bordeaux, or a forty-minute drive on the A62 highway.

ADDRESS

Château Doisy Daëne
15 Gravas
33 720 Barsac

CONTACT

+33 (0)5 56 62 96 51
denisbourdieu.fr

54 ACRES
(22 ha) including

40 ACRES
(16 ha) of vines

Expertise

Founded in the early eighteenth century in the hamlet of Doysy, this château had several owners—including Jean Jacques Emmanuel Daëne, a Bordeaux wine merchant of English extraction—before being acquired in 1924 by Georges Dubourdieu, a winegrower in Illats. His grandson, Denis Dubourdieu, who passed away in 2016, was a distinguished figure in Bordeaux, known for his contributions to agronomy and oenology. A professor at Bordeaux's university and vice president of the Institute of Vine and Wine Science, he was a recognized expert on the process of white winemaking and the various phenomena associated with fermentation and bottle aging.

EMOTION

Technique may be essential, but it is nothing without emotion: "When we love a wine that is just right, with a flavor that reflects its origins," Denis Dubourdieu would say, "we absorb the landscapes, culture, and history of the place where it was conceived, the personality and the philosophy of the people who made it." Doisy Daëne wines have an aromatic wealth, concentrated flavor, and ethereal balance that perfectly express this winemaking philosophy, to which the fourth generation of the Dubourdieu family, Fabrice and Jean Jacques, are more dedicated than ever.

THE EXTRAORDINARY "L'EXTRAVAGANT"

The idea for this prestige vintage came about shortly before the 1990 harvest, when Denis Dubourdieu planned to attempt "a pure Sauvignon with a concentration of noble rot pushed to the very limit." It proved to be a complex undertaking, but Dubourdieu worked closely with his father to ferment a must of incredible richness, and obtained a wildly successful result that sold for more than any other Bordeaux white wine—Yquem included. Subsequent vintages included varying proportions of Sémillon, but the wine lost none of its legendary status.

VINEYARDS

The Château Doisy Daëne vineyard covers about 40 acres (16 ha) located between Climens and Coutet. Like most of the Barsac plateau, the terroir is made up of sand and clay soil over a limestone bedrock that limits the impact of dry spells by forming a water reservoir. The vineyard is primarily planted with Sémillon (86 percent) and includes several plots of Sauvignon (13 percent) and Muscadelle (1 percent). Average vine age is forty years.

TOURS & TASTINGS

Visitors are invited to tour the cellars, and vegetable and beekeeping gardens, followed by a tasting in the boutique of three wines from the family properties. Reservations are recommended during the week and essential on weekends.

TASTING 3 wines

PRICE €€

2007 2007
SAUTERNES
Château
Doisy Daëne

68

CHÂTEAU CLIMENS

PREMIER GRAND CRU CLASSÉ, BARSAC

The Lord of Barsac

The name "Climens" appears on a contract from 1547, when Guirault Roborel, the king's advocate in Barsac, acquired his first plots of land here. Of Frankish origin, the word refers to land too poor for ordinary crops and therefore perfect for exceptional wines! The current château—a simple seventeenth-century country house—was embellished with two square turrets in the late eighteenth century. After the phylloxera epidemic in the late nineteenth century, the château's vineyard was entirely replanted by Henri Gounouilhou, a newspaper manager and the son of a leading printer from Bordeaux, who made Climens the most elegant of the Barsacs and the only wine to credibly rival Château d'Yquem.

GETTING THERE

Château Climens is located about twenty-five miles (40 km) south of Bordeaux, or a forty-minute drive from the town center on highway A62.

ADDRESS

Château Climens
33 720 Barsac

CONTACT

+33 (0)5 56 27 15 33
contact@chateau-climens.fr
chateau-climens.fr

74 ACRES
(30 ha) of vines

CHATEAU CLIMENS
1er CRU
HAUT - BARSAC

Soucis
Millepertuis
Romarin
Camomille
Pissenlit
Achillée
millefeuille

SIGNATURE

In 1971, Château Climens was acquired by Lucien Lurton, a prominent Bordeaux winegrower; his youngest daughter, Bérénice, took over in 1992. The composition of varietals and the surface area of the vineyard have remained the same for at least two centuries, despite the château changing hands several times—a rare phenomenon among Bordeaux's grands crus. In 2010, the château adopted a biodynamic approach for the entire vineyard and is unique for being the only premier cru in Bordeaux to be certified biodynamic. These efforts are intended to strengthen the already distinctive identity of the wine. Bérénice Lurton readily describes it as a world apart from other Sauternes, and from Bordeaux wines in general, with its marriage of nuance and liveliness.

VINEYARD

The château's four enclosed plots, encircled by stone walls typical of Barsac, span seventy-four acres (30 ha) and are entirely planted with Sémillon. The terroir features red, iron-rich sandy clay that forms a layer a little less than three feet (1 m) deep over a gently sloping bedrock of fissured Stampian limestone, providing the ideal conditions for this unique wine.

TOURS & TASTINGS

Slow Tasting Tour
Extend a classic tour of the vineyard, wine cellar, and *tisanerie*, where plant-based vineyard treatments are prepared, with this in-depth tasting. Take your time and savor the sensory pleasures of Château Climens Asphodèle, the château's first dry white wine, and Cyprès de Climens, the second wine, as well as three Château Climens vintages.
TASTING 6 wines
PRICE €€€€

Meditation and Yoga
You'll need to find at least three companions for this activity, but it is well worth it: after a tour and before a tasting paired with a light, refined lunch, you'll be treated to a vine-themed session of yoga and relaxation in the lovely *tisanerie*. An incredible experience not to be missed if you visit the château between May and September.
PRICE €€€€ (minimum 3 participants)

FOOD & DRINK

Dining at Climens
If you're visiting in a group of at least four, and you would like to indulge in an outstanding gastronomic meal with bold pairings featuring several of the château's great vintages, book a lunch in Climens's private dining rooms.
PRICE €€€€ (minimum 4 diners)

CIRON
GARONNE
A62
CHÂTEAU DE MALLE
CHÂTEAU ROMER
CHÂTEAU ROMER DU HAYOT
66
CHÂTEAU RABAUD-PROMIS
72
63
65
CLOS HAUT-PEYRAGUEY
61
62
CHÂTEAU RIEUSSEC
77
CHÂTEAU LAMOTHE-GUIGNARD
69
CHÂTEAU LAMOTHE
CHÂTEAU FILHOT
0
1km
½ mile

SAUTERNAIS

SAUTERNES

- 61 Château d'Yquem
- 66 Château Suduiraut
- 69 Château Guiraud
- 63 Château Lafaurie-Peyraguey
- 72 Château Sigalas Rabaud
- 65 Château de Rayne Vigneau
- 77 Château d'Arche
- 62 Château la Tour Blanche

61

CHÂTEAU D'YQUEM

PREMIER GRAND CRU CLASSÉ SUPÉRIEUR, SAUTERNES

A legendary wine
Château d'Yquem is at once a legend, a miracle of nature, and a wine like no other. Open a bottle of Yquem and time stands still. Yquem has universal charm; it moves the heart, soul, and senses of everyone who tastes it.

GETTING THERE

To reach Château d'Yquem, take the A62 highway south of Bordeaux and get off on the third exit (Tarbes, Pau, Langon), then take the D8 highway heading toward Sauternes.

ADDRESS

Château d'Yquem
33 210 Sauternes
CONTACT
+33 (0)5 57 98 07 07
yquem.fr

SIGNATURE

Château d'Yquem is an extraordinary place, nestled atop the rolling hills of Sauternes, with 272 acres (110 ha) of vineyards planted across a mosaic of terroirs. Everything is in place to produce a grape that brings out the most noble aspects of *Botrytis cinerea*. The fruit undergoes a complex process that leaves it laden with flavors and aromas found nowhere else in the world. This miracle is made possible by the dedication of experienced harvesters who have received age-old knowledge from the generations that preceded them. Only the best grapes, enhanced by *Botrytis cinerea*, are harvested, in accordance with Yquem's golden rule: never take the easy path or seek shortcuts and be prepared to lose everything. That's the price to pay for excellence.

A harvest of meticulously selected grapes sets the stage for cellar vinification that requires very little input. Barrel aging is longer and adapted to the rhythm of the wine. The result must be perfection: here, it's Yquem or it's nothing at all.

AURA

For centuries, Château d'Yquem has been served at the grandest celebrations and to the world's most illustrious figures: from European kings to Russian czars to Japanese emperors. Epicureans and wine enthusiasts throughout the ages have always held this legendary elixir in the highest regard. The world's best chefs serve Yquem in their restaurants and even create specifically tailored dishes in the quest for an incomparable pairing. These restaurants are beacons, projecting Yquem's light into the world.

Yquem's aura shines beyond the realm of gastronomy; it has been hailed by great statesmen like George Washington and was named Premier Cru Classé Supérieur following Napoleon III's 1855 request for classification. Château d'Yquem also inspires artists, sparking emotions in musicians, painters, poets, and writers. French writer Frédéric Dard described Yquem as "light that one drinks."

465 ACRES
(188 ha) including

272 ACRES
(110 ha) of vines

80% Sémillon
20% Muscadelle

VINEYARD

The Yquem estate is located on the slopes found along the right bank of the Céron River. Covering 465 acres (188 ha) in total, it is both the most prestigious and the largest estate in Sauternes. The uninterrupted vineyard spans three hilltops over 272 acres (110 ha), and is planted with Sémillon (80 percent) and Muscadelle (20 percent) on gravel soil over a foundation of clay.

TOURS & TASTINGS

Since 2018, the château has offered exclusive tours for up to six visitors, by reservation only. A visit to Château d'Yquem is a voyage through four hundred years of history and an exploration of an estate where art and craftsmanship unite to create a unique wine.

Discovery
This private, guided tour is followed by a tasting of Y 2018 and Château d'Yquem 2018.
TASTING 2 wines
PRICE €€€

Trilogy
Following a visit of the vineyard and winemaking facilities, you will taste three recent vintages of Château d'Yquem (2018, 2017, and 2016).
TASTING 3 wines
PRICE €€€

Anthology
Following a tour of the estate, discover the heights of a legendary wine, with a tasting of three outstanding vintages of Château d'Yquem: 2015, 2009, and 2001.
TASTING 3 wines
PRICE €€€€

66

CHÂTEAU SUDUIRAUT

PREMIER GRAND CRU CLASSÉ, SAUTERNES

GETTING THERE

Château Suduiraut is located less than thirty miles (50 km) south of Bordeaux, or about a forty-five-minute drive on the A62 highway.

ADDRESS

Château Suduiraut
33 210 Preignac

CONTACT

+33 (0)5 56 63 61 92
suduiraut.fr

Le Cru du Roy

Although the château—which was included in the French Inventory of Intangible Cultural Heritage—was renamed Le Cru du Roy by Baron Jean Joseph Duroy, a nephew of the Suduiraut family, it respects all the conventions of the highest aristocracy: a foundation dating back to the late sixteenth century, light-filled architecture typical of the seventeenth century (the first château was destroyed during the Fronde insurrection), and magnificent gardens designed by French landscape architect André Le Nôtre.

SIGNATURE

Sémillon predominates in the grand cru blend, where Sauvignon Blanc keeps a low profile: the balanced result arises from skillful work with characteristics found in the estate's various micro-terroirs. The wine is aged in oak casks for eighteen to twenty months.

Château Suduiraut has belonged to AXA Millésimes since 1992. Pierre Montégut, a sweet-wine enthusiast with a comprehensive knowledge of noble rot, has been technical director since 2004. "*Botrytis* cannot be managed," he explains. "Its progress must be monitored carefully through constant observation in the vineyard. The challenge lies in beginning the harvest at the right moment." And much is at stake: the team must wait long enough for the grapes to attain sufficient maturity and concentration of sugars, but intervene in time to preserve the fruit's aromatic clarity and acidity, and limit the risks of inclement weather in October. Harvesters go through the vineyard up to five times to identify which clusters are ready to be picked. The château is so exacting that no *grand vin* is bottled in years when the quality of the harvest is deemed inadequate.

TRADITION

The winemaking process at the château showcases the Bordeaux tradition, using spur pruning that exposes the clusters of fruit to the sun and helps concentrate aromas in the grapes. Ploughing is carried out with both mechanical and manual methods, and only organic fertilizers are used. At pressing time, the team demonstrates care and patience to protect the aromatic brightness of the juice intended for vinification. Each cask is closely monitored during fermentation to preserve the rich aromas produced by the jammy botrytized fruits.

VINEYARD

The 225-acre (91-ha) vineyard, which received High Environmental Value certification from the French Ministry of Agriculture, is planted with 90 percent Sémillon and 10 percent Sauvignon Blanc. Average vine age is thirty-five years. The terroir includes sandy clay gravel at altitudes between 82 and 164 feet (25–50 m), with the highest point located at Château d'Yquem, and there is a spring that supplies the château.

225 ACRES
(91 ha) of vines

90% Sémillon
10% Sauvignon Blanc

TOURS & TASTINGS/WORKSHOPS

Château Suduiraut offers private tours by appointment only, followed by a tasting of its *grand vin* and its second wine.

Wine and Cheese Workshop
This workshop gives you the chance to taste three fine vintages of Château Suduiraut. A variety of cheeses has been carefully selected to bring out the freshness of the 2014, the complexity of the 2006, and the brightness of the 2000.
DURATION 1½ hours
TASTING 3 wines
PRICE €€€

Aromas Workshop
After visiting the winery, you will enter a beautiful tasting room where staff will introduce you to the characteristic aromas of this premier cru classé. Two activities are available with this workshop:

Discover the Aromas of Sauternes
For this option, you can choose between two pairs of this grand cru classé: 2014 and 2006, or, if you would like to travel further back in time, 2006 and 2000.
DURATION 1½ hours
TASTING 2 wines
PRICE €€€

Château Suduiraut Masterclass
This enjoyable tour includes a vertical tasting of three grands crus classés. You'll learn to identify individual aromas and match them to those presented in the workshop.
DURATION 1½ hours
TASTING 3 wines
PRICE €€€

69

CHÂTEAU GUIRAUD

PREMIER GRAND CRU CLASSÉ, SAUTERNES

Natural excellence
Intimate, bucolic, and welcoming, this château has put biodiversity to work for oenological excellence. The château's Sauternes owes its aromatic complexity to a fine-tuned partnership with nature. In 2011, Château Guiraud distinguished itself as a pioneer among other premiers grands crus classés when it qualified for the esteemed "organic" certification. Today more than ever at Château Guiraud, the implementation of the principles of permaculture encourages a holistic approach, in which the property as a whole is taken into consideration, including the vines, woods, amenity trees, park, and buildings.

GETTING THERE

Château Guiraud is located about thirty miles (50 km) from Bordeaux, or about a forty-minute drive, on the Bordeaux Wine Route (D2 highway) in Graves and Sauternes.

ADDRESS

Château Guiraud
33 210 Sauternes

CONTACT

+33 (0)5 56 76 61 01
chateauguiraud.com

SIGNATURE

Grass is allowed to grow naturally in this vineyard to support soil life, protect surfaces from erosion, and conserve heat. Hedges run along the vines, providing homes for an impressive microcosm of more than six hundred species of insects, spiders, earwigs, bees, and ladybugs, each playing its role in protecting the grapes and helping them thrive. These creatures also provide essential support to *Botrytis cinerea*, the scientific name for noble rot: a mold that grows on wine grapes and gives these wines their unique identity.

Maintaining this balance requires a heavy dose of science and hard work, but it is all worthwhile. The château's many visitors particularly appreciate this relationship with the earth and its undeniable influence on the quality of this grand cru classé.

40,000 VINES
grafted and planted every year

316 ACRES
(128 ha)

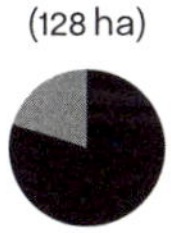

comprised of **80%** sandy gravel

VINEYARD

The entire landscape on these ancient terraces formed by the Garonne River has been shaped through thirty years of work to restore the soil's microbial diversity, establish a complex ecosystem, and reduce ploughing to a minimum. Sandy gravel comprises 80 percent of the estate's 316 acres (128 ha); the remaining areas present a combination of limestone and heavy clay. The vineyard's relatively high altitude provides the perfect amount of ventilation for encouraging noble rot just when the grapes of this terroir, known for producing early harvests, are ripe.

BIODIVERSITY AT EVERY LEVEL

In 2001, Château Guiraud established a conservatory with more than 135 Sémillon and Sauvignon Blanc rootstocks, which enables the estate to maintain and keep a record of the genetic diversity of on-site *cépages*, as well as to graft and plant forty thousand grapevines each year.

A biodiversity garden in the heart of the vineyard invites visitors of all ages to discover a large variety of vegetable plants, as well as different shelters designed to accommodate insects and birds, who help protect against pests.

FOOD & DRINK

La Chapelle, the on-site restaurant, is a must for gourmets eager to discover new Sauternes pairings. The menu features organic vegetables from the château's garden.

TOURS & TASTINGS

Discover the Vineyard
This fascinating tour includes a comprehensive presentation of the estate, fermenting room, and wine cellar, followed by a tasting.
DURATION 1½ hours
TASTING 3 wines
PRICE €€

Take an Aromatic Journey
Awaken the sommelier within by selecting three vintages yourself to create a vertical tasting. Discover even more about the history of an estate that has proudly gone its own way since 1766.
DURATION 1½ hours
TASTING 3 wines
PRICE €€

Explore the Vineyard by Bicycle
Electric bicycles are available to explore the entire vineyard and enjoy several points of interest and panoramic views. This hard-to-resist option includes a wonderful garden-inspired picnic.
DURATION 3–7 hours
PRICE €€€

Caviar in the Spotlight
Château Guiraud works with ethical, sustainable caviar producers to offer its most discerning visitors a superior pairing experience.
DURATION 2 hours
TASTING 1 wine
PRICE €€€

63

CHÂTEAU LAFAURIE-PEYRAGUEY

PREMIER GRAND CRU CLASSÉ, SAUTERNES

A secular history

The word "château" is particularly fitting for Lafaurie-Peyraguey, which is located on the site of a medieval stronghold, near Yquem. The château's entrance, surrounding wall, and towers, constructed in the thirteenth century, are thought to be the oldest stones in the commune of Bommes. There is evidence that a branch of the Peyraguey family lived in Bommes and dates the estate's creation to 1592–94. The first vineyards were planted here by the family in 1618. Several generations of Peyragueys would follow in their footsteps.

GETTING THERE

Château Lafaurie-Peyraguey is located about thirty miles (50 km) from Bordeaux, or about a forty-minute drive on the Bordeaux Wine Route (D2 highway) in Graves and Sauternes.

ADDRESS

Château Lafaurie-Peyraguey
Lieu-dit Peyraguey
33 210 Bommes

CONTACT

+33 (0)5 24 22 80 11
chateau-lafaurie-peyraguey.com

SAUTERNES IS THE MOST EMOTIONAL WINE IN THE WORLD. BEHIND THE SAUTERNES WINE THAT EVERYONE KNOWS, THERE IS ALSO A MAGNIFICENT REGION AND A PEOPLE WITH STRONG VALUES.

—SILVIO DENZ

46 ACRES
(18.5 ha) of vines

93% Sémillon
7% Sauvignon Blanc

ART

In 2014, a new chapter began when the château was purchased by Silvio Denz, owner of French glassmaker Lalique, two grands crus classés in Saint-Émilion, and three other properties in the Bordeaux region. The engraving *Femme et Raisins* (Woman with Grapes) depicting a female figure surrounded by grapes, created by René Lalique in 1928, continues to inspire Denz and has appeared on the estate's bottles and crates since the 2013 vintage. The chapel nestled between the château's two cellars features a red marble altar designed by Pietro Mingarelli. Today, the structure houses Lalique's most beautiful historic and contemporary works.

VINEYARD

The 46-acre (18.5-ha) vineyard is located on the high gravel terrace of Sauternes, 230 feet (70 m) above sea level. The L'Enclos and Les Maisons Rouges parcels form the historical core of this fine terroir composed of Quaternary gravel deposited over six hundred thousand years ago on a substrate of Aquitanian limestone. Sémillon dominates the vineyard, although Sauvignon and Muscadelle are present in modest quantities.

CHÂTEAU LAFAURIE-PEYRAGUEY
1618
2018
1ER GRAND CRU CLASSÉ - SAUTERNES

FOOD & DRINK/ CHÂTEAU STAYS

Lalique Hotel and Restaurant
In 2018, the château celebrated its four-hundredth anniversary by opening the first hotel-restaurant located on the grounds of a grand cru classé. Initiated by Silvio Denz, the establishment aims to unite fine dining, wine, crystal, and hospitality. After receiving a first Michelin star in 2019—providing Sauternes with its first Michelin-starred restaurant—chef Jérôme Schilling and the Lalique Restaurant were awarded two stars by the Michelin Guide in March 2022. The five-star hotel features thirteen immensely elegant rooms and contains a beautiful library replete with books about the history of Sauternes and Bordeaux wines, the vineyards, and René Lalique and his works.

La Terrasse de Lafaurie
Relax and enjoy a unique menu inspired by world cuisine and featuring a number of dishes cooked over a grill fed with vine shoots, prepared before you by chef Alejandro Moyo, a longtime collaborator of Jérôme Schilling. Open for lunch only, from beginning May to end September.

Dinner in the Vineyard
This unforgettable experience offers the opportunity to enjoy the cuisine of the château's two-Michelin-starred restaurant, served at a table in the midst of Château Lafaurie-Peyraguey's vineyards—a truly exceptional moment in an unparalleled setting.
PRICE €€€

TOURS & TASTINGS

Classic Tour
Dive into the history of Château Lafaurie-Peyraguey and Sauternes to discover the secrets of making sweet wine. After visiting the estate, fermenting room, cellars, and chapel, you will taste three of the château's vintages. Also available as a private tour with a tasting of four vintages.
TASTING 3–4 wines
PRICE €€€

Tour and Vertical Tasting
This tour includes a visit of the estate and its winemaking facilities, followed by a vertical tasting of four vintages of the premier grand cru classé. Open up your taste buds to the magic of Sauternes and discover what makes each vintage unique.
TASTING 4 wines
PRICE €€€

Food and Wine Pairing Visit
BY JÉRÔME SCHILLING
Whet your appetite and curiosity with this tasting by the talented, Michelin-starred chef Jérôme Schilling. Savor bite-size pairings served with three of the château's wines during a memorable guided tasting.
TASTING 3 wines
PRICE €€€

Five-Star Scooter Tour
Meet at 9:30 a.m. at the Au Fil du Ciron adventure park in Bommes for a two-and-a-half-hour tour of five of the most renowned vineyards in the region: Rayne-Vigneau, La Tour Blanche, Sigalas-Rabaud, Rabaud-Promis, and, of course, Château Lafaurie-Peyraguey. Rest assured—you're scheduled to stop at one of these five châteaux for a tasting!
DURATION 2½ hours
PRICE €€€

72

CHÂTEAU SIGALAS RABAUD

PREMIER GRAND CRU CLASSÉ, SAUTERNES

Unrivaled hospitality
With a mere thirty-five acres (14 ha) of vineyard near the Ciron River, this estate managed by Laure de Lambert Compeyrot is one of the smallest grands crus classés, but it is also one of the oldest, and undoubtedly one of the most welcoming. The château's tradition of hospitality earned it first place in the Best of Wine Tourism 2022 awards by Great Wine Capitals in the Accommodation category.

GETTING THERE

Château Sigalas Rabaud is located about thirty miles (47 km) south of Bordeaux, or a forty-minute drive on the A62 highway.

ADDRESS

Château Sigalas Rabaud
33 210 Bommes

CONTACT

+33 (0)5 57 31 07 45
chateau-sigalas-rabaud.com

HISTORY

The Rabaud estate dates back to the seventeenth century and was acquired by Henri de Sigalas in 1863. His son sold two-thirds of the property forty years later, keeping only the gravelly, south-facing hilltop, which he called "the jewel of Sigalas." His granddaughter, Marie Antoinette de Sigalas, Marquise de Lambert des Granges, took up her grandfather's pursuit of excellence in 1949. Her son, Gérard, Marquis de Lambert des Granges, a living encyclopedia of Sauternes history, speaks of the vine as a capricious and compelling partner. His feeling is understandable, when you consider that Sauternes are among the most challenging wines to vinify, not least because of the difficulties inherent in managing noble rot and the risk of harvesting overripe grapes.

VINEYARD

These thirty-five unbroken acres (14 ha) are located near the Ciron River, on clay bedrock. The sandy-gravel soil deposited by the Garonne River six hundred thousand years ago provides the vines with the perfect nourishment. The vineyard is predominantly planted with Sémillon, with a small portion reserved for Sauvignon.

SIGNATURE

Laure de Lambert Compeyrot carries on her family's tradition of developing this incomparable terroir by applying environmentally responsible methods of pest control. She pours her efforts into making a more natural wine, even going so far as to abandon production of her *grand vin* when the vagaries of the weather prohibit harvesting the grapes in their ideal state, which she describes as "roasted, wrinkled, shriveled, hairy, rotten, and delicious," illustrating with concise beauty the paradox of Sauternes's excellent wines.

FOOD & DRINK

La Terrasse de Sigalas
This setting invites you to pause to enjoy the view of the vineyard, while indulging in a selection of fine products specially chosen to be perfectly paired with the château's wines.
Open 10 a.m.–7 p.m.
PRICE €€–€€€

35 ACRES
(14 ha) of vines

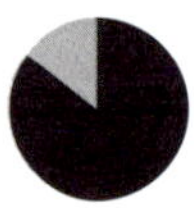

85% Sémillon
15% Sauvignon Blanc

TOURS & TASTINGS

Sigalas Discovery
Discover the history of Château Sigalas Rabaud during this tour of the winemaking facilities, complete with a tasting of three wines in an exceptional setting.
DURATION 30 minutes
TASTING 3 wines
PRICE €

Sigalas's Secrets
Visit the *chartreuse* and take in the unique panorama of the most beautiful vineyards of Sauternes, before discovering the secrets behind winemaking at the château. The tour ends with a tasting of three wines.
DURATION 1 hour
TASTING 3 wines
PRICE €€

Gourmet Sigalas
This tour will whet your appetite as you explore the vineyard and the cellar, then taste three wines, followed by a gourmet platter served with a glass of Sauternes under the château's red parasols, facing the magnificent view.
DURATION 2½ hours
TASTING 3 wines and gourmet platter
PRICE €€€€

Sigalas Coffee
During this unique experience, you'll taste the first coffee to be aged in Sauternes barrels: an Ethiopian arabica, carefully selected and certified organic, aged for nine weeks at the château.
PRICE €€

Timeless Sigalas
Come and meet the Marquis de Lambert des Granges, a man of culture and tradition. He will share with you his knowledge about his wine, and Sauternes and Bordeaux AOCs, before you partake in a tasting of four vintages of the premier cru classé.
DURATION 2 hours
TASTING 4 wines
PRICE €€€

65

CHÂTEAU DE RAYNE VIGNEAU

PREMIER GRAND CRU CLASSÉ, SAUTERNES

The treasures of a terroir
This estate, founded in the early seventeenth century by Gabriel du Vigneau, received premier cru classification thanks to the efforts of Catherine de Pontac, Baroness of Rayne, who acquired it in 1834. Her grand-nephew, Albert de Pontac, gave the château its current name. Château de Rayne Vigneau, currently owned by the Trésor du Patrimoine group, is managed by Vincent Labergère, assisted by Guillaume Rateau.

GETTING THERE

Château de Rayne Vigneau is located about thirty miles (50 km) south of Bordeaux, or an hour's drive on the A62 highway.

ADDRESS

Château de Rayne Vigneau
4 Le Vigneau
33 210 Bommes

CONTACT
+33 (0)5 56 76 64 05
raynevigneau.fr

SIGNATURE

The soil in the vineyard is renowned for containing a wealth of amethyst, sapphire, and onyx swept down from the Pyrenees mountains hundreds of thousands of years ago. Legend has it that these gemstones contribute to the grand cru's deep, shimmering color.

The estate closely adheres to the Sauternes tradition, harvesting in multiple runs so that not a single grape is picked before it has been sufficiently transformed by the magical *Botrytis cinerea*, or noble rot. Four to eight sessions of manual sorting may be necessary, depending on how *Botrytis* is progressing through the vineyard. Wines are aged for eighteen months in oak barrels, 30–40 percent of which are renewed each year.

Concerned with limiting its impact on nature, Château de Rayne Vigneau uses only plant-based products for its wines, and it received the French Ministry of Agriculture's Level Three High Environmental Value certification: a guarantee that the estate's agricultural practices, which produce one of the appellation's most dependable wines, also preserve the ecosystem and reduce the château's environmental impact to a minimum.

207 ACRES
(84 ha) of vines

74% Sémillon
24% Sauvignon Blanc
2% Muscadelle

VINEYARD

Covering 207 acres (84 ha), the Château de Rayne Vigneau vineyard is located on a fine hilltop near the town of Bommes, overlooking Sauternes. The clay and gravel soil contains semiprecious stones from the Pyrenees mountains. The vineyard is planted with 74 percent Sémillon, 24 percent Sauvignon Blanc, and 2 percent Muscadelle. The vines are, on average, thirty years old.

TOURS & TASTINGS/ WORKSHOPS

Discovery Tour and Tasting
Discover the history of this beautiful estate and the characteristics of its terroir, as well as the secrets of vinification, followed by a tasting of three wines. Reservation optional.
DURATION 1 hour
TASTING 3 wines
PRICE €€

The Secrets of Rayne Vigneau
This expanded version of the Discovery Tour culminates in a vertical tasting of three Château de Rayne Vigneau vintages, from the most recent to 2009.
DURATION 1 hour
TASTING 3 wines
PRICE €€€

The Great Vintages Experience
Travel through twenty years of this prestigious château's history during a tasting of six vintages of the *grand vin*, from the most recent to 2002.
DURATION 1½ hours
TASTING 6 wines
PRICE €€€

The Sweet Escape
This Sauternes-themed escape game begins in the château's dining room. Use your powers of logic and observation to solve a series of riddles and crack the codes to hunt down a mysterious stone and discover the role it plays in crafting this premier cru wine.
DURATION 1½ hours
TASTING 3 wines
PRICE €€€

Awake the Five Senses Workshop
This fun workshop offers an unusual introduction to tasting by engaging all five senses. It's a perfect way to fully experience the château's three wines.
DURATION 1½ hours
TASTING 3 wines
PRICE €€€

Blending Workshop
This practical workshop will teach you how varietals are selected for blending—and you'll leave with your very own custom premier grand cru wine.
DURATION 2½ hours
PRICE €€€€

Tasting on a Tree Top
Grab your harness and get ready for a professional to hoist you into a two-centuries old cedar tree. There, you will taste the château's grand cru, and thrill to the sight of the incredible panorama.
DURATION 2½ hours
TASTING 3 wines
PRICE €€€€

Sauternes on Scooters
This tour, introduced in 2022, invites you to discover the "Five Stars of Sauternes" by electric scooter, before tasting three Château de Rayne Vigneau wines.
DURATION 2 hours
TASTING 3 wines
PRICE €€€

77

CHÂTEAU D'ARCHE

DEUXIÈME GRAND CRU CLASSÉ, SAUTERNES

Fostering connection and exchange

Château d'Arche is one of the most popular destinations among visitors to Sauternes, and quite rightly. Perched on the hill that rises between Sauternes and Haut-Bommes, above the Ciron valley, the estate dates back to the seventeenth century, but was renamed in 1733 when it was purchased by the Count of Arche. Confiscated and carved up during the French Revolution, the property was not restored to its original configuration until after World War I. Château d'Arche was acquired by an investment group in 1996; since then, environmental concerns and a commitment to hospitality have been central to its long-term vision.

GETTING THERE

Château d'Arche is located about twenty-five miles (40 km) southeast of Bordeaux, or a forty-minute drive on the A62 highway.

ADDRESS

Château d'Arche
33 210 Sauternes

CONTACT

+33 (0)5 56 76 67 67
chateau-arche.fr

SIGNATURE

The château's hotel, offering magnificent views, and the ISO 14001 and Level 3 High Environmental Value certifications it holds attest to its conscientious approach to hospitality and environmental issues. Its ecological commitment is further demonstrated through its ongoing conversion to organic farming and the construction of an 8200-square-foot (2,500-m²) eco-responsible cellar, which was inaugurated in 2019.

The cellar is equipped with thirty-three stainless steel vats with a capacity of 370 barrels. Clad in siding made of acacia wood—the same material used to make the vineyard stakes—it blends into the landscape. The building, whose green roof limits the amount of energy expended on temperature regulation, also features a system for recycling rainwater and wastewater. The cellar architect, Benoît Sacaze, designed the facility to be a modern, high-performance tool, with a layout that invites visitors on an immersive journey from vine to glass in order to better appreciate the scope, breadth, and depth of this grand cru.

The members of the team at Château d'Arche work hand in hand to make Château d'Arche a center of œnological excellence focused on connection and sharing. Visitors travel here from around the world to stimulate their taste buds and their minds.

VINEYARD

The vineyard covers 210 acres (85 ha), including seventy-four uninterrupted acres (30 ha) reserved for Sauternes. The terroir comprises starfish limestone and light gravel at its highest point, clay soil on the slopes, and fine silt at the foot of the hill. The vineyard's roots plunge up to thirty-three feet (10 m) in certain places. The vineyard is planted with 85 percent Sémillon and 15 percent Sauvignon Blanc.

CHÂTEAU STAYS

Hôtel du Château d'Arche
A pioneer in wine tourism in Sauternes, the château opened the first hotel in the region to be located on a winemaking estate in 2002. The hotel's eight rooms provide an exceptional view over one of the most beautiful vineyards in the world. The three-star hotel will appeal to anyone who loves wine, nature, and fine cuisine, and caters for short and long stays.
PRICE €€€€

210 ACRES
(85 ha) of vines

85% Sémillon
15% Sauvignon Blanc

TOURS & TASTINGS

The Classic Visit: The Secrets of Château d'Arche, 1855 Grand Cru Classé
Take a tour of the facilities and discover the secrets of making a Sauternes grand cru classé, before tasting three of the château's wines.
DURATION 1 hour
TASTING 3 wines
PRICE €€

Vertical Tasting
Discover how time influences wine. The tour ends with a vertical tasting of four vintages to give you a better understanding of and appreciation for the way the château's wines have evolved over the years.
DURATION 1½ hours
TASTING 4 wines
PRICE €€€

French *Art de Vivre*
The team at this epicurean château wouldn't dream of letting its guests leave on an empty stomach. Visitors are invited to enjoy a glass of wine served with a selection of cheeses, charcuterie, and other local products.
PRICE €€

Wine and Golf
Château d'Arche offers "athletic" visitors and the curious a chance to discover a winemaking estate from another perspective. Make yourself comfortable in the old cellars and explore the most beautiful golf courses in the world on a professional Trackman simulator. A one-of-a-kind experience in France, this tour is open to everyone.
PRICE €€€

The Art of Aging
Château d'Arche is more than a vineyard—it is a lively hub of encounters and exchanges. The château has therefore partnered with VIP Wines & Spirits to immerse guests in the art of aging. The casks that are so important for winemaking are given a second life when they are later used to age spirits; Château d'Arche and VIP Wines & Spirits have joined forces to introduce guests to these two not-so-different worlds. This tasting includes a selection of spirits from VIP Wines & Spirits.
PRICE €€€

Other activities
→ Electric bicycles are available for half-or full-day rentals.
→ Château d'Arche can be privatized for events such as weddings and conferences.
→ The château also hosts a series of lively events every Sunday, from May to October.

Reservations can be made on the château's website. Follow the château on Instagram for regular updates about events and activities.

62

CHÂTEAU LA TOUR BLANCHE

PREMIER GRAND CRU CLASSÉ, SAUTERNES

A visionary project
Several memorable individuals have left their mark on the history of this château, beginning with Monsieur de La Tour Blanche, a court clerk in the Parliament of Bordeaux, who inherited the property in the early eighteenth century. Later, the wine merchant and Consul of Oldenburg Frederick Focke purchased the estate, and contributed to establishing practices that are now second nature in Sauternes, such as late harvesting carried out in several runs. Tragically, Focke died in 1855, several weeks before his efforts were rewarded and his château included in the 1855 Classification as a premier grand cru.

GETTING THERE

Château La Tour Blanche is located about twenty-five miles (40 km) southeast of Bordeaux, or a forty-minute drive on the A62 highway.

ADDRESS

Château la Tour Blanche
33 210 Bommes
CONTACT
+33 (0)5 57 98 02 73
tour-blanche.com

CHATEAU · LA · TOUR · BLANCHE

A BEQUEST TO MARK THE HISTORY OF THE CHÂTEAU

In 1876, another visionary, Daniel Iffla, acquired the estate. Of modest origins, he made his fortune in finance and used his wealth to fund many philanthropical endeavors. After purchasing Château La Tour Blanche, he enlisted the help of Louis Pasteur and the biochemist Ulysse Gayon to help him better understand the role of microorganisms and microfungi in winegrowing and winemaking. Upon his death in 1907, he bequeathed the château to the French State, on the condition that a winegrowing and oenology school be established there. His wishes were granted in 1911. Château La Tour Blanche has belonged to the Nouvelle-Aquitaine region since 2010. The region's public agricultural school offers several training programs in wine-related professions. In addition to playing an educational role, the estate's winemaking activities are managed entirely by professionals who have the expertise to ensure the continued success of this grand cru classé, reputed for its balance of power and freshness.

VINEYARD

The vineyard culminates at 220 feet (67 m) above sea level, on a slope overlooking the Ciron River. Ninety-one of its ninety-nine acres (37 of its 40 ha) are located within the Sauternes appellation, and are planted with 83 percent Sémillon, 12 percent Sauvignon, and 5 percent Muscadelle. The terroir at the top of the slope, composed of gravelly soil over a bedrock of clay, gradually transitions to a layer of sand over a limestone bedrock.

TOURS & TASTINGS

Discovery Tasting
The tour begins with a historical presentation in the courtyard of the château, followed by a visit to the vineyards (weather permitting), where you will discover how the vines in Sauternes are maintained. You will climb the château's belvedere to take in an exceptional panoramic view, before ending the tour with a tasting of three Sauternes wines produced by the château.
DURATION 1½ hours
TASTING 3 wines
PRICE €€

Vertical Tour
This option can be added to the preceding tour and includes a tasting of three vintages of the grand cru classé, so that you may appreciate how it evolves over time.
DURATION 1½ hours
TASTING 3 wines
PRICE €€

So'Affinés Tour
After exploring the vineyard, ascending the belvedere, and visiting the château's winemaking facilities, you will be given a detailed explanation of the vinification process in the fermenting room and barrel cellar. This exceptional tour ends with a tasting of perfectly matched wine and cheese: three of the château's Sauternes are paired with four cheeses that have been aged and selected by the on-site master cheesemaker.
DURATION 1½ hours
TASTING 3 wines and 4 cheeses
PRICE €€

BORDEAUX GRANDS CRUS CLASSÉS 1855

ESSENTIAL INFORMATION

"The best wine is not necessarily the most expensive,
but the one that you share." —**GEORGES BRASSENS**

ALL ABOUT WINE

TIPS FROM AN EXPERT

BY ÉRIC BEAUMARD
Manager of the restaurant Le Cinq ✪✪✪
World Vice-Champion Sommelier, and Best Sommelier in France and Europe

TASTING

The goal of tasting wine, even when a very fine cru classé is involved, is not to be intimidated, but to enjoy the experience, to enrich your olfactory palate, and to savor a special occasion, whether by yourself or with friends or family. The following tips are meant to guide your approach to the world's finest wines. They will help you distinguish nuances and appreciate the incredible complexity of grands crus.

TASTING A SAUTERNES

Sweet white wines should be consumed at a temperature between 54°F and 57°F (12°C–14°C) to allow them to fully express themselves. Don't be afraid to serve them on the cool side: they will warm up a little in the glass. The visual inspection is one of the great pleasures of drinking a Sauternes or Barsac. A neutral, ideally white backdrop is best for analyzing color, which varies from pale green-gold in the youngest wines to amber in the oldest.

A Sauternes's initial nose (before the glass is swirled) will allow you to determine if it is closed, subtle, or open, depending on the intensity of the aromas.

A wine's aromatic complexity is evaluated along with its intensity: after swirling the wine in the glass, take a series of short breaths to saturate and desaturate your olfactory receptors. These wines present primary aromas of fruit (roasted peach, quince, pineapple), and the presence of Sémillon may contribute notes of beeswax and hazelnut. Less opulent Barsacs are often characterized by a pleasant freshness.

Finally, take your first sip in order to appreciate the wine's flavors and aromas. Sauternes are evaluated first on their balance between freshness (or acidity), sugar, and alcohol as compared with the appellation, and, perhaps more importantly, on how long the often intense aromas linger in the mouth.

TASTING A MÉDOC

If you are about to taste a Médoc between three and five years old, decant your bottle at least two hours ahead of time, to let the wine breathe. Decanting will also eliminate any natural deposits that may have formed in the bottle. A shorter period, around thirty minutes, is enough to decant a Médoc that has been kept for ten years or more, as long as you are careful to treat it gently, to avoid stirring in too much oxygen (by virtue of their powerful structure and the presence of tannins, Bordeaux's *grand vins* can be decanted without losing any of their complexity). Temperature is another important factor: ideally, Bordeaux should be consumed at a temperature of 60°F–64°F (16°C–18°C).

The deep, jewel tones of Médoc red wines are undeniably pleasant to behold. They may have violet or dark brown accents, or possibly sparkle with purple or garnet. Wine reveals its texture in the way that it clings to the sides of the glass, forming more or less fluid drops, depending on how much body it has.

A Médoc's nose will strike you with its combinations of sous-bois (forest floor) fruits, spices, and flowers, and it might be interesting to try to discern the characteristics of the individual grape varieties used in the blend. Keep in mind that a strong proportion of Merlot tends to enhance aromas of black fruits and floral notes.

Take a mouthful of wine. Once you've picked out the Cabernet Sauvignon tannins, try to identify the flavors of each grape variety present. Don't forget to evaluate how short-lived or lingering the flavor is.

FOOD AND WINE PAIRING

Food and wine pairing is complex and deserves consideration. Here are a few rules to remember to create successful pairings, from classic to unusual combinations.

AN AFICIONADO'S GUIDE TO FINE BORDEAUX WINE

VADE MECUM

Renowned for the diversity of the vintages and their incredible aging capacity; eighty-seven Bordeaux Grands Crus Classés vintages are summarized below. These notes are drawn from the archives of the Tastet & Lawton bureau de courtage, which has assessed the vintages since its foundation in 1740.

QUALITY OF VINTAGES SINCE 1900

0–9 mediocre
10–12 average
13–14 pretty good
15–16 good
17–18 very good
✪ **19–20** excellent

Vintage	Red	Sweet white
2019	18	17
✪2018	19	18
2017	16	17
✪2016	19	17
✪2015	18	19
2014	16	13
2013	12	12
2012	16	14
2011	16	18
✪2010	19	18
✪2009	19	19
2008	18	18
✪2007	16	19
2006	18	16
✪2005	19	18
2004	17	16
✪2003	18	19
2002	16	15
✪2001	19	18
2000	18	15
1999	16	15
1998	17	16
✪1997	15	19
1996	18	17
1995	17	15
1994	15	13
1993	14	12
1992	12	11
1991	13	13
✪1990	19	19
✪1989	19	18
1988	17	17
1987	14	14
1986	18	18
1985	18	15
1984	12	13
1983	17	18
✪1982	19	16
1981	16	16
1980	13	14
1979	16	15
1978	17	14
1977	11	17
1976	16	17
1975	17	16
1974	12	9
1973	12	10
1972	10	8
1971	17	17
1970	18	18
1969	12	12
1967	14	17
1966	17	14
1964	17	14
1962	17	18
✪1961	20	19
1960	12	11
✪1959	19	18
1958	12	11
1957	12	10
1956	9	8
✪1955	18	19
1954	9	9
✪1953	18	19
1952	17	17
1950	16	16
1949	12	9
1948	15	11
✪1947	18	19
1946	10	10
✪1945	19	18
1944	10	8
1943	17	17
1942	11	13
1940	13	13
1939	12	10
1938	12	12
1937	17	20
1934	17	17
✪1929	20	19
✪1928	19	17
1926	18	17
1924	17	17
1921	18	18
1920	16	15
1906	16	15
1904	16	14
✪1900	20	20

WINE BOTTLE FORMATS

CONTAINER SIZE
AND EQUIVALENTS

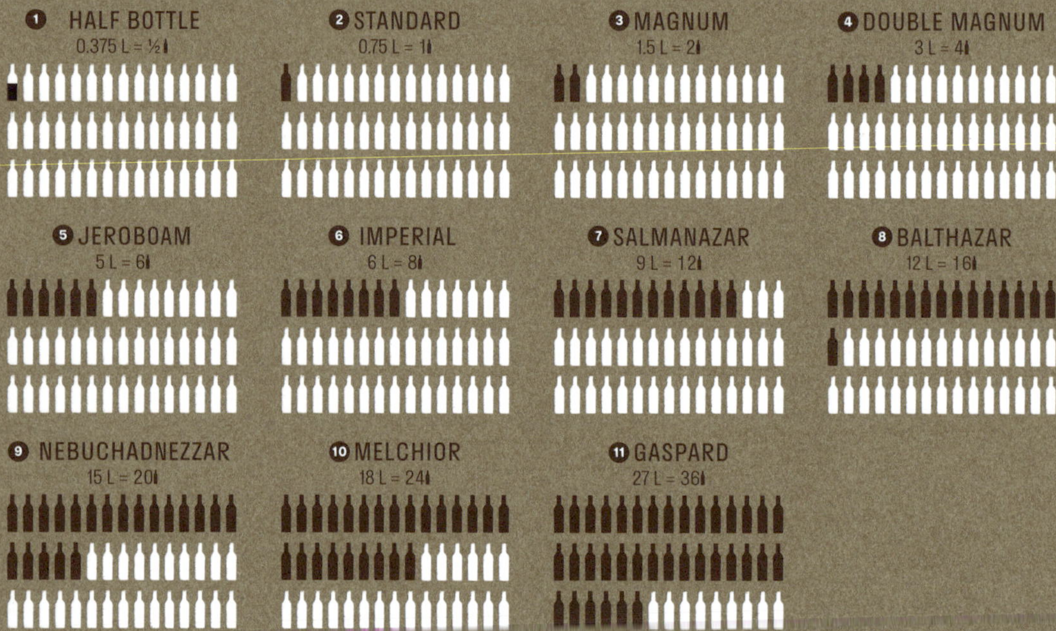

- Be attentive to the order in which you serve the wines throughout the meal, and never risk serving a wine that would make you wish you were still drinking the previous one.
- A chilled Sauternes grand cru served as an aperitif is a real delight.
- Wines generally pair well with dishes from their region of origin.
- Sauternes and Barsac go wonderfully with cheese, particularly Roquefort and other blue-veined varieties.
- Red wines from Médoc are suited to lamb and duck breast.
- Spicy dishes call for light, refreshing wines.
- Supple, light red wines are appropriate with white fish, but are not recommended with rare, red meats.

STORING WINE

While many grands crus classés can be enjoyed young, they can all be aged and should be stored with care. How you preserve wine will fundamentally influence its evolution over time.

Protect your bottles from light and vibration by storing them in an odorless, well-ventilated area with an ambient humidity of 75 percent and a temperature between 55°F and 59°F (13°C–15°C). If you don't have a home cellar, you can purchase a freestanding cellar specifically designed for aging wines. In any case, store your bottles horizontally—the cork must remain in contact with the wine to keep it from drying out and shrinking, and to prevent oxidation.

TIP

If you don't want to decant your wine, place the bottles vertically in the cellar the night before you intend to drink them to keep deposits from forming. Be gentle when serving.

A BOTTLE FOR EVERY OCCASION

The aging process varies depending on the size of the bottle. Be aware that the larger the bottle, the better it will age. Why? Oxidation and redox, the reactions responsible for aging, take place faster when the ratio of air to liquid is higher. If you want to acquire a fifteen-year-old vintage and are able to, choose the largest bottle!

WHY 750 ML?

Bottle size is linked to the history of trade between Bordeaux and England. To facilitate conversions between the two countries' units of measure during the purchasing process, Bordeaux's barrels were designed to carry 225 liters of wine, a volume equal to approximately 50 English imperial gallons, which works out to a practical three-hundred 750 ml bottles (that's twenty-five cases of twelve bottles, to be exact.)

You may come across older bottles with a 730 ml capacity. This is because the space occupied by the cork was not officially counted until the nineteenth century, and the change led to a modification in bottle volume.

THE ART OF BLENDING

Blending is fundamental to creating Bordeaux wines. Merlot, Cabernet Sauvignon, Cabernet Franc, and Petit-Verdot in Médoc, and Sauvignon Blanc and Sémillon in Sauternes are cultivated on specific plots and generally fermented separately, which requires distinct winemaking processes. When fermentation is complete, the cellar master proceeds with blending by carrying out a series of tests and blind tastings of different proportions to identify those that will best express a given vintage.

1855 ART AND WINE

BY KAREN TAYLOR

The wines of the 1855 Classification are among the most famous in the world, often lauded as veritable works of art. Yet while winemakers are sensitive to the many resonances between the worlds of art and wine, they are quick to point out that winemakers are not artists.

Frédéric Rouzaud, owner of **CHÂTEAU PICHON COMTESSE DE LALANDE** and creator of the Fondation Louis Roederer, believes the term "contemporary artisan" is more appropriate. "Every year, we endeavor to craft a new wine, one that respects tradition but that is a wine of tomorrow, that corresponds to the tastes of tomorrow. Artists inspire us in that work, and our support of the arts sends a message that we appreciate beauty and the search for beauty, that we seek to surpass ourselves rather than simply repeat ourselves."

Châteaux throughout the Médoc and Sauternes share this vision, communicating their aspirations through dazzling architecture, contemporary art exhibitions, and site-specific commissions. These artistic choices are highly individualistic, highlighting the unique character of each of these storied châteaux.

Great architecture, like great wine, can elicit excitement, awe, and emotion. Château owners have long understood that the combination of the two can be powerful indeed. The first estate to enlist the talents of a celebrated architect was **CHÂTEAU LAFITE ROTHSCHILD**, which in 1988 hired Ricardo Bofill to redesign its barrel-aging room. Revolutionary at the time, the circular design checked all the right boxes for the most advanced winemaking techniques and efficient workflow. As for the aesthetics, they are breathtaking even today: sober columns and strict geometry suggest a Greek temple, and subtle lighting imparts a quasi-religious atmosphere.

A wave of winery renovations followed, all driven by a similar imperative to incorporate high-performance facilities within an architectural framework that would underscore the estate's prestige. Among the most notable was **CHÂTEAU BARON PICHON LONGUEVILLE**, whose 1989 revamp by Jean de Gastines and Patrick Dillon called for a vaulted concrete vat room and cellars installed beneath a reflecting pool mirroring the fairy-tale nineteenth-century château. Then in 2008, **CHÂTEAU COS D'ESTOURNEL** stole the architectural spotlight when it unveiled its *new chai* designed by Jean-Marie Wilmotte. Boasting every high-tech bell and whistle, it looked like a cool stage set for a James Bond movie. The wine world had never seen anything quite like it.

Each of the many designs of that period was radically different, but nearly all had one thing in common: they did not modify the exterior appearance of an estate's buildings. That approach has changed in recent years, the result of additions to the architect's brief: winemakers now want to give visitors memorable—and Instagrammable—experiences, and they want to convey their deep connection to nature and the environment.

Two landmark designs completed in 2015 illustrate these new directions. At **CHÂTEAU MARGAUX**, Norman Foster took on the challenge of creating of-the-moment winemaking facilities and visitor areas while not detracting from the centerpiece of the estate: the magnificent neo-Palladian château that is now a classified historic monument. An agricultural village is located to one side of the château, and Foster's elegant solution was to house an ultramodern facility beneath a pitched roof whose shape and tiles blend seamlessly with the adjacent historic buildings. Sculptural tree-like structures support the roof, evoking the rows of majestic plane trees lining the entrance to the château. Inside, glass walls flood the vat room with natural light and provide the tasting room with views of Margaux's legendary vineyards. Every detail, from the 230 foot-long (70 m) display of rare bottles to the stainless-steel spiral staircase, is the ultimate expression of twenty-first century technology and aesthetics informed by a respectful sense of place.

At Pauillac's **CHÂTEAU PÉDESCLAUX**, Jean-Marie Wilmotte had far fewer restraints. The estate was run down, and the new owners wanted a total transformation of their "sleeping beauty." Together they decided that luminosity and transparency would drive the design, reflecting Pédesclaux's commitment to wine that requires minimal intervention. The result was the addition of dramatic, two-story glass wings on either side of the original stone château, which now houses reception spaces, tasting areas, and guest rooms. Wilmotte also created a handsome, gravity-fed vat room from scratch, taking the iconoclastic approach of placing the building above ground and incorporating glass walls.

That same year, **CHÂTEAU GRUAUD LAROSE** scored a Médoc first when Lanoire & Courrian built a large addition conceived uniquely for visitors. A spacious reception area, boutique, and tasting room are housed in a low-slung building that opens onto the restored park and gardens. The showstopper is the twenty-first-century spin on the classic château tower: a double staircase encased in stainless-steel mesh walls rises some seventy feet (21 m) into the air, arriving at viewing platforms that provide 360 degree panoramas of the Gruaud Larose vineyards and surrounding landscapes.

Fabulous views are also to be had at one of the latest additions to the Pauillac skyline: the new winery at **CHÂTEAU LYNCH-BAGES**, completed in 2020. Designed by Didi Pei (son of architect I.M. Pei of Louvre Pyramid fame), it is a striking glass-and-stainless steel structure that adds much needed space while incorporating the latest technologies and ergonomic design. Bathed in natural light, the building is also extremely energy efficient, with treated glass and screens that eliminate the need for air conditioning. A tasting room and spaces for art exhibitions were added with visitors in mind, as was the spiral staircase that leads to a viewing deck offering vistas that extend to the Garonne estuary.

When it comes to the environment, the most audacious project to date is unfolding at **CHÂTEAU CANTENAC BROWN**, famous for its lovely Tudor-style château. Working with architect Philippe Madec, a pioneer in sustainable development, Cantenac Brown is building a state-of-the-art winery that will be carbon neutral. The walls and vaulted ceiling (the only one of its size in Europe) are being made out of blocks of compressed clay and sand by using a technique that dates back a thousand years. All building materials are locally sourced, no cement is used, and no air conditioning will be needed.

Major construction projects are planned for nearly a dozen more grand cru châteaux, from Pauillac to Sauternes. The next chapter in winery architecture is about to be written.

Contemporary art made a shaky début in the Médoc in 1923, when Baron Philippe de Rothschild commissioned graphic artist Jean Carlu to create a painting for **CHÂTEAU MOUTON ROTHSCHILD**'s wine label. His idea was to call attention to the fact that wine was now being bottled at the château instead of the *négociant's* warehouse. While innovations in the vineyards and cellars were always applauded, deviating from the traditional labels was considered un peu trop. The Baron reluctantly abandoned the Carlu design after a few years.

His vision was nonetheless vindicated two decades later when he asked Philippe Jullian to illustrate the label for the 1945 vintage celebrating the Allied victory in World War II. It was an immediate success, and to this day Mouton invites a different talent—Miró, Chagall, Braque, Bacon, Koons, Haring—to create the label for each vintage. In 1981, these famous illustrations were put on display at the château and were so popular that they eventually toured some forty countries. The Paintings for the Labels room, on view and updated every year, is one of the Médoc's most popular attractions.

No other château has tried to compete with Mouton's labels (understandably so), but they do occasionally call on artists to help them celebrate special events

↑
Château Lynch-Bages
Pauillac

or occasions. In 2009, Karl Lagerfeld illustrated the label marking the three hundred and fiftieth anniversary of Chanel-owned **CHÂTEAU RAUZAN-SEGLA**. Two years later, jewelry designer Jade Jagger created a sexy black-and-gold label for the launch of Croix de Beaucaillou, the second wine of **CHÂTEAU DUCRU-BEAUCAILLOU**. Most recently, **CHÂTEAU HAUT-BAGES LIBÉRAL** selected a work by renowned printmaker and garden designer François Houtin for its new CERES cuvée, the first Pauillac grand cru that is totally organic and natural with no added sulfites.

While Mouton houses the only permanent collection of contemporary art, a number of other châteaux host temporary exhibitions, most often as a form of sponsorship. Paintings and sculptures may be displayed in vat rooms, aging cellars, reception areas, gardens, or parks, adding a rich layer to the experience of visiting these châteaux. Whether the works are by local or international artists, the quality is generally quite high, making these events great opportunities for collectors in search of fresh talent.

Among the pioneers is **CHÂTEAU LYNCH-BAGES**, whose first showing of contemporary art took place in 1989. For many years, the château has partnered with Paris's esteemed Galerie Lelong, making it possible to bring exciting artists—Antoni Tàpies, Hervé Di Rosa, Pierre Alechinsky—to the Médoc. The gallery-like spaces in Lynch-Bages's new winery are sure to enhance the prestige of these widely anticipated events.

CHÂTEAU BEYCHEVELLE is another longtime champion of the arts. In 1990, the estate launched an ambitious International Center of Contemporary Art that unfortunately was short lived. Temporary exhibitions continue, however, and it is difficult to imagine a more glorious backdrop for contemporary sculpture than this stunning eighteenth-century château with its majestic park and gardens leading down to the Garonne. The cellars, renovated in 2017, offer yet another spectacular setting, with their sleek stainless-steel fermentation tanks and architectural features inspired by the tall-masted ship featured on the château's famous label.

Art lovers will also want to check out the exhibition calendars at Margaux's **CHÂTEAU D'ISSAN**, where every other year owner Virginie Cruse showcases works by French and international talents with a connection to Bordeaux. Nearby **CHÂTEAU LASCOMBES** presents a wide range of regional art—one recent show featured outsized metal sculptures, another presented intricate paintings on oak staves recovered from wine barrels. **CHÂTEAU MARQUIS DE TERME**, meanwhile, has a year-round calendar of cultural events, including exhibitions of French and international artists who are invited to stay at the château and become personally involved in mounting their solo shows.

CHÂTEAU PALMER has taken a somewhat different tack, opting to present world-class photography during its annual exhibitions. The château has hosted such masters as the legendary Brazilian photographer Sebastião Salgado, jazz photographer Guy Le Querrec, and award-winning Magnum photographer Raymond Depardon. Exhibition themes vary, but a frequent leitmotif is the environment and the impact of climate change around Bordeaux and around the world.

In a recent twist, new construction and renovations are influencing the grand cru art scene, with owners seeking out major works to complement their château's arresting architecture while also reflecting its winemaking philosophy. **CHÂTEAU PÉDESCLAUX**, for example, has commissioned several large-scale canvases from Fabrice Hyber, an artist known as much for his passionate defense of the environment as for his sculptures, paintings, installations, and videos exhibited in museums throughout the world.

In Sauternes, **CHÂTEAU LAFAURIE-PEYRAGUEY** has taken this concept to another level, boldly putting art at the very center of its recent renovations. Owner Silvio Denz, who also owns Lalique, drew on the crystal company's extensive archives to inspire what is now the first luxury hotel and Michelin-starred restaurant in the appellation. The interior architecture and furnishings are fresh and contemporary, perfect foils for René Lalique's art deco designs. Throughout the estate, crystal artfully accents furniture, lighting, accessories, mirrors, and doors. Even the Lafaurie-Peyraguey bottle has been given an elegant frosted-crystal inset, surely a grand cru first.

Those looking for a glimpse into the future of art at these venerable estates need look no further than **CHÂTEAU CANTENAC BROWN**. To highlight the construction of its revolutionary raw-earth winery, owner Tristan Le Lous asked artist David Popa to create a piece of land art on the property using only natural pigments, earth, and water. As planned, the monumental fresco washed away with the rain but not before it was preserved by photographs, videos taken by drones, and an NFT sold through cryptocurrency. Rarely has ephemeral art left such a lasting impression.

KAREN TAYLOR
is the former editor of *France Magazine,* published by the French-American Cultural Foundation. She now writes about cultural topics for various publications and institutions.

THE CGCC AND THE FRAC

For many years, nonprofits such as the FRAC (Fonds Régional d'Art Contemporain) Aquitaine have solicited grand cru châteaux for their support, asking that they open their historic properties to artists and visitors. Whenever possible, owners respond with enthusiasm and generosity. In 2016, the Bordeaux-based FRAC demonstrated its gratitude for these enduring collaborations when it exhibited ephemeral abstract works by Nicolas Boulard made entirely from soil samples taken from all eighty-seven grand cru châteaux. The CGCC/FRAC partnership continues to this day: In 2021, Margaux châteaux Kirwan, Marquis d'Alesme, Siran, Issan, and Giscours sponsored FRAC exhibits designed to help local artists affected by the pandemic.

ARTFUL PAIRINGS

Throughout its history, the CGCC has always embraced art and artists, as well as great wines. As part of the 1989 exhibition *Bordeaux Châteaux* at Paris's Georges Pompidou Center, English painter Carl Laubin created an original work of art that fancifully wove together illustrations of the façades of all eighty-seven châteaux. It was made into a poster that became hugely popular.

In 2008, the CGCC asked Yann Arthus-Bertrand, one of the greatest French photographers and president of the GoodPlanet Foundation, to imagine a second CGCC poster. His clever response was to combine photographs of each of the eighty-seven grand cru bottles held by a human hand—his way of paying tribute to the men and women who work behind the scenes to produce these legendary wines.

A decade later, the CGCC invited rock-star designer Philippe Starck to take his turn at paying tribute to the grand cru châteaux. As always, his solution was original and seductive: using complex computer graphics, he immersed the viewer in the colors and movement of the wine itself, while suggesting the grand theatricality of a stage curtain that is about to rise.

A GREAT WINE
IS ONE
OF THE MOST
ADMIRABLE
CONSTRUCTIONS
OF ATOMS
KNOWN TO MAN.

—PHILIPPE STARCK

MÉDOC

THE MÉDOC'S MANY TERROIRS

BY CORNELIS VAN LEEUWEN
Professor of Viticulture
at ENITA, Bordeaux

Terroir plays a major role in the reputation of 1855 grands crus classés. The word itself encompasses more than soil quality; it refers to an ecosystem in which land, climate, and vine interact. It is the connection between the final product and its geographic origin.

As far back as Roman times, certain high-quality wines were linked to the place where they were grown. In Bordeaux, this idea of connection has existed since the Middle Ages, when certain wines were valued for and sold under the name of the town where they were produced. Estate wines emerged in the seventeenth century, when Haut-Brion was the first premier cru to sell its production under the château's name. This led to a more precise definition of a wine's terroir and origins, now defined by a property's several tens of acres and no longer by a town's thousands of acres. The English market played a decisive role in this process: its consumers were ready to pay high prices for fine wines.

AN ENLIGHTENED PHILOSOPHER

The account of John Locke's trip to the region in 1677 gives us an idea of what people knew about the importance of terroir at that time. The trip was a pilgrimage of sorts, for the famous philosopher had been so impressed by the Haut-Brion wines he tasted in London that he wanted to know more and set out to visit the property. There, he learned that the quality of the wines was due to a natural environment of meager soils and sloping hillsides, and vineyard practices that included low manure use and old vines. The elements that are now recognized as essential to growing quality wine had been identified more than three centuries ago.

SOIL

Soils in Médoc are incredibly diverse and present a variety of textures, gravel content (the local word for inert, silicious pebbles is graves), mineral fertility, water content, and depth. No one type of soil is "best," as Professor Seguin, from the Œnology Department at the Institute of Vine and Wine Science in Bordeaux, reminds us, but certain characteristics appear essential to producing quality fruit.

A soil's capacity to retain water has a clear influence on the quality of a wine. The best results are obtained when water supply is limited in summer. This interrupts the growth of branches and produces smaller grapes, which encourages concentration. And because these soils tend to shed water, they warm quickly in spring and limit temperature drops at night, which supports ripening.

CLIMATE: A DETERMINANT FACTOR IN TERROIR

Vine growth and fruit maturation are heavily dependent on climatic conditions like temperature, precipitation, sun, humidity, and wind. The vineyard is also sensitive to excessive heat and weather events, like hail (a rare occurrence in Médoc) and frost in spring, which can destroy a year's worth of work in a matter of hours.

With an average annual temperature of 55°F (13°C), and 68°F (20°C) in July and August, the climate in Médoc is perfectly suited to the vine. Temperature variations are limited by the region's proximity to the Atlantic Ocean and the Gironde estuary, which protects crus classés from spring frosts. In 1991, a year memorable for the disastrous frost that struck Bordeaux on the night of April 20, those crus classés located along the Gironde, like Château Latour, were spared and produced wines of a surprising quality for the vintage.

Since irrigation is all but banned in France, rainfall is also decisive. With an average precipitation of 33 ½ in. (850 mm), Médoc has a rainfall level slightly higher than the ideal required to obtain a maximum of concentration in the grapes, but this slight excess is compensated by permeable soils with good drainage.

THE VINTAGE EFFECT

Bordeaux's climat (a combination of geography and weather conditions) varies considerably from year to year, which has a direct influence on the quality and flavors typical of the region's wines, depending on the year the grapes were harvested. This is called the "vintage effect." In a way, wine provides a record of past weather conditions. For example, it was warm and sunny in 1945 and 1947, two exceptional vintages, and more recently in 2003 (a heat wave year), 2005, and 2009, while it rained significantly in 1963 and 1965, years when most of the château owners refused to sell even a drop of that year's wine, too diluted and bad to be sold under their names. Vintage also refers to producing a different wine for the same cru each year, while maintaining the château's style. In a way, each vintage highlights a different facet of the cru at each harvest. Cool years, like 1978, 1988, and 2013, when the grapes were slow to ripen and harvested late, supported finesse in the wine's aromatic expression. Hot years, like 1982, 1989, 1990, and 1995, or more recently 2003, 2005, 2009, 2010, 2015, 2016, and 2018 make for strong wines. It's interesting to note that all the great vintages are characterized by lower-than-normal rainfall in the months between June and September.

CÉPAGES (GRAPE VARIETIES)

The 1855 grands crus classés are obtained by blending different grape varieties together: Cabernet Sauvignon, Merlot, Cabernet Franc, and Petit Verdot. Their success is explained in large part by the complementary relationship between these early-ripening grape varieties and Bordeaux's climate. These factors support good fruit maturity (except in exceptionally cold years like 1972), while maintaining a long ripening period that contributes to a wine's finesse.

CABERNET SAUVIGNON

Cabernet Sauvignon is the most noble of all grape varieties and most often forms the backbone of red 1855 crus classés. It is relatively late to ripen and must be reserved for the best soils, which accelerate maturation. It produces a moderate and fairly steady harvest of small fruits and clusters. This variety does not have the capacity to reach high concentrations of sugar, but the ripe fruit is colorful and rich in tannins. Cabernet Sauvignon produces aromatic wines dominated by black fruits (currant) when young, which, as they age, can reach unparalleled levels of complexity, with a flavor palate that includes notes of cacao and mint.

MERLOT

Merlot is almost always a necessary complement to Cabernet Sauvignon. It may occupy up to a third of cultivated land (Haut-Brion and Pichon-Longueville Comtesse de Lalande) and, although uncommon, it may be present in quantities equal to Cabernet Sauvignon (Palmer). Merlot ripens about two weeks earlier than Cabernet Sauvignon, which means it tends to reach a satisfactory level of maturation every year, even in cool years, when Cabernet Sauvignon may have difficulty reaching maturity. Merlot performs well in moist soils that take longer to warm up. But for this variety to fully express its qualities, its natural richness must be controlled. Merlot produces sweet, colorful grapes with supple tannins. Aromas dominated by red and black fruit in young wines evolve towards candied fruit, leather, and fur as the wines age.

CABERNET FRANC

The third most common red grape variety cultivated in Bordeaux, Cabernet Franc is more popular in the Libournais than in Médoc, for reasons that have yet to be explained. It reaches maturity somewhere between Merlot and Cabernet Sauvignon. Endowed with great potential to achieve finesse, it is sometimes criticized for its lightness. However, excellent Cabernet Franc is obtained by certain crus classés from very old vines planted in very good soil.

PETIT VERDOT

Although planted in smaller proportions, Petit Verdot plays an important role in certain vintages. It is a late-ripening variety, and therefore difficult to master each year. As global warming advances, we can expect to see an increase in land planted with Petit Verdot in the years to come.

SAUTERNES

EXCELLENCE: THE ORIGINS OF SAUTERNES

Boasting the most premiers crus and the only premier cru supérieur in the 1855 classification, the wines of Sauternes and Barsac are rooted in a long tradition of excellence. Sauternes' terroir has gained a reputation progressively, stemming from the production of a wine made from noble rot grapes.

The miracle of terroir: this is the only region in the world where the microscopic fungus *Botrytis cinerea*, or noble rot, enhances grapes rather than destroying them. This "gray mold" concentrates sugars and aromas in the fruit. In return, harvests, which extend from October to late November, must be carried out with extreme care and expert hands.

SOILS

Sauternes has two distinct terroirs. On the right bank of the Ciron, where the towns of Sauternes and Bommes are located, lies an east-facing plateau. Its limestone and sandy clay bedrock was covered with croupes, or hills, of gravel during the quaternary period, swept along by the Garonne. These pale soils capture the sun's heat and protect the vineyard from frost. The vines must send their roots to depths of more than 30 feet (10 m) to access necessary nutrients.

On the left bank of the Ciron, on the Barsac side, the red soils are strewn with large gravel pebbles and rest on a fissured and permeable plateau of starfish limestone. Here, roots travel through a layer no more than 1½ feet (50 cm) deep to colonize the limestone.

CLIMATE

Sauternes' microclimate owes much to the interactions between the cold waters of the Ciron (cooled as it travels more than 60 miles [100 km], sheltered by a thousand-year-old oak forest) with those of the Garonne, between Barsac and Preignac. In fall, as the cooler water runs into the warmer water, it creates a mist that hangs over the vineyard from dawn to midday. Drying breezes limit the effects of noble rot and protect the grapes.

CÉPAGES: (GRAPE VARIETIES)

SÉMILLON

Sémillon is emblematic of Sauternes, where it thrives like nowhere else. The grape's fine skin facilitates the development of noble rot. This variety gives the wines their roundness and extraordinary aromatic breadth.

SAUVIGNON BLANC

This grape variety is very present in dry white wines and is used in blends to contribute freshness and minerality.

MUSCADELLE

Particularly difficult to grow, Muscadelle complements Bordeaux's sweet white wines by bringing a floral character with notes of honeysuckle and acacia.

SAUTERNES: A TRADITION OF WHITE WINES?

BY STÉPHANIE LACHAUD[1]

It seems indisputable that the reputation of the Sauternes terroir was built on the production of wine made with noble rot grapes, a fact attested to by numerous archival documents. In Sauternes, the first mention of this wine appeared on October 10, 1657, in Barsac.

In his *Traité sur la nature et la culture de la vigne* (Treatise on the Nature and Culture of the Vineyard) published in 1759, agronomist Nicolas Bidet[2] mentions late harvests as the distinguishing factor by which Sauternes white wines are recognized.

"Among the sweet wines are, without doubt, those from Barsac, Preignac, and Langon: their sweetness is particular in that not only is it mixed with much strength or spirit, but it remains and increases over time. But these are not en primeur wines, which is to say they are not sold in the first season, either because they were harvested late, or because they improve in the cellars and fetch a higher price when they are older. When kept for thirty years, this wine becomes equal or superior to wines from Spain, the Canary Islands, and Malaga, and they are known as late-harvest wines, as are those wines that are only sold around the month of March or later."

The presence of sweet white wines in Sauternes in agronomic literature suggests the extent to which the reputation of Sauternes, Barsac, and Preignac is tied to this type of wine. This knowledge also appears in the observations of many enlightened connoisseurs. In his *Travel Diaries*, Thomas Jefferson recounts his trip to Sauternes in late May of 1787. "Sauterne [sic] is the pleasantest, next Prignac [sic], and lastly Barsac. But Barsac is the strongest, followed by Prignac, and lastly Sauterne. And all are stronger than Grave [sic] .... Near Langon is Sauterne, where the best white wines of Bordeaux are made."

That the capital's elite, as well as foreign travelers like Jefferson, consumed these sweet white wines is confirmation that a wine's reputation was dependent on the reputations of those who drank it—that is, until the 1855 Classification formalized a definition of production. Carried out with the support of the Broker's Union in Bordeaux, the classification was presented as the reflection of reality at that time, based on the price of wines, and established standards of quality and taste for the winemaking region of Sauternes.

These various criteria confirm the existence of a high-quality winemaking tradition of sweet white wines. They also attest to a long social and historical process in which wines are the expression of a particular social milieu. Indeed, when Jefferson continues his description of Sauternes vineyards, he identifies the best crus in each parish: "1. Sauterne, the best crop belonging to Monsieur d'Yquem at Bordeaux."

The production of sweet white wines strongly characterizes the winemaking region of Sauternes, but the sought after "nectar" was obtained with more or less success each year. Certain châteaux began using late-harvest techniques and sorting in the eighteenth century, while more modest estates had to content themselves with rather late harvesting to obtain a bit of sweetness. The tradition of sweet white wines that established the reputation of Sauternes appears to be a historical construction long in the making. Today, this production is a powerful marker of identity, but remains a fundamentally social and cultural fact that reveals the importance of know-how and history in the construction of a wine-growing region.

---

1. STÉPHANIE LACHAUD
Associate Professor, Modern History
Université Bordeaux
Montaigne, France
Author of *Le Sauternais moderne. Histoire de la vigne, du vin et des vignerons des années 1650 à la fin du XVIIIe siècle* (Bordeaux: Fédération Historique du Sud-Ouest, 2012) and several other books about vineyards and wine.

2. NICOLAS BIDET
Traité sur la nature et la culture de la vigne, vol. 2 (Paris: Savoye, Libraire, 1759), 267.

SHOULD YOU FINISH AN OPENED BOTTLE OF SAUTERNES?

BY FABRIZIO BUCELLA[3]

One of the little known advantages of grands crus classés from Sauternes and Barsac is their exceptional resistance to the effects of air.

Oscar Wilde claimed that "to know the vintage and quality of a wine one need not drink the whole cask." Does this adage apply to sweet grands crus? In other words, if you open a bottle of Sauternes and Barsac, do you have to finish it within a matter of days? Or can you enjoy it for several weeks?

How can you determine if the opened bottle can be kept in the refrigerator? By performing an air resistance test (see p. 234). We tested the air resistance of Sauternes and Barsac 1855 crus classés. To create the most common conditions, the research was carried out using an appliance found in every home: the domestic refrigerator. The experiment described below should reassure readers that consuming a bottle of Sauternes and Barsac over a lengthy period will not alter the remaining product.

Traditionally, the resistance test is carried out on wine that is left in contact with air for a period of one to five days. Observations of appearance, smell, and taste indicate the wine's behavior, aging potential, or possible fragility. We multiplied this interval by seven, testing the air resistance of Sauternes and Barsac 1855 crus classés for up to five weeks (thirty-five days) preceding tasting.

AIR RESISTANCE TEST

The air resistance test is carried out as follows. The experimenter observes the evolution of the wine remaining in an open bottle. They carry out a complete sensory analysis. They note if the wine remains crystalline, fresh, and balanced. They pay attention to floral and fruity notes, and evaluate any traces of oxidation in order to verify if exposure to air has damaged the wine's structure.

EXPERIMENT PROCEDURE

Six bottles of the 2016 vintage of the same Sauternes and Barsac 1855 cru classé and its second wine were selected by the oenology school Inter Wine & Dine in Brussels. In week zero (the beginning of the experiment), a calibrated quantity of liquid (c. 7 fl. oz./21 cl) was extracted from bottle no. 1, which was then recorked and placed vertically in the door of the refrigerator. During the second week, the same operation was carried out with bottle no. 2. The experiment proceeded in this manner until the fifth week. At this point, the experimenter had six bottles that had been opened at one-week intervals; the final bottle was opened just before tasting. A complete sensory analysis of all twelve wines (*six grands vins* and *six seconds vins*) was carried out in order to assess air resistance.

TASTING

The wines were tasted by six experts, all members of the œnology school Inter Wine & Dine. They evaluated seven indicators commonly used to describe Sauternes and Barsac wine. Each taster evaluated the following indicators on a scale of 1 (totally absent) to 10 (very present): fresh fruit, candied fruit, spicy, woody, honey, caramel, and oxidized notes (for example, warm or rotten apple or dry nuts). At the end of the experiment, the average ranking was calculated for each indicator and graphed on a radar chart (see Sensory Analysis on facing page).

A TRICK TEST FOR A GOOD CAUSE

In order to verify the panel's skill, we included two of the same samples in the tasting. The idea was to see if different notes were given to identical samples. Fortunately, this was not the case, confirming the consistency of the judges' responses.

RESULTS

The wines' aromatic structure remained the same, regardless of when the bottle was opened (at one week intervals for five weeks). So there is no notable organoleptic difference between wines subjected to various levels of oxidation. A Sauternes and Barsac 1855 cru classé opened four to five weeks preceding the moment of consumption cannot be distinguished from the same wine opened just before tasting. What's more, there is no difference in the presence of flavors indicative of oxidation between bottles opened at different times.

Time does not appear to radically affect the structure of Sauternes and Barsac 1855 grands crus classés. Bottles no. 1 and no. 6, opened five weeks apart, performed equally on several criteria. During the tasting, no wine seemed to have deteriorated during its time in the refrigerator, once the bottle had been opened.

CONCLUSION

The results of the experiment are indisputable. Sauternes and Barsac 1855 grands crus classés show no perceptible organoleptic difference, even when the bottle is opened five weeks before tasting. In the minds of the tasters, they are drinking the same wine. This is true of both the *grands* and *seconds vins*. Consequently, it is entirely reasonable to keep an open bottle of Sauternes and Barsac 1855 grand cru classé in the refrigerator door for up to five weeks.

To return to Oscar Wilde, you can indeed enjoy a Sauternes and Barsac 1855 cru classé without drinking the entire cask.

3. FABRIZIO BUCELLA
Account of an experiment carried out by Professor Bucella and his teams at the Free University of Brussels, Belgium.

SENSORY ANALYSIS

SIX WINES FROM SAUTERNES
AND BARSAC OVER TIME

GRAND VIN

2016 VINTAGE

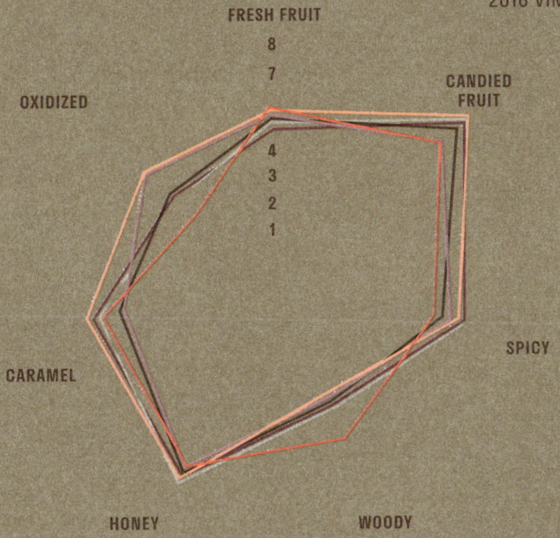

	SPICY	WOODY	HONEY	CARAMEL
Week 0	6.5/10	4.5/10	7.25/10	7.25/10
Week 1	5.25/10	5.5/10	6.75/10	6.75/10
Week 2	6.25/10	3.75/10	7/10	7/10
Week 3	5.5/10	4/10	7/10	7/10
Week 4	5.75/10	4/10	7/10	7/10
Week 5	6.5/10	4/10	7/10	7/10

	OXIDIZED	FRESH FRUIT	CANDIED FRUIT
Week 0	3.5/10	4.5/10	8/10
Week 1	2.5/10	5/10	7/10
Week 2	5/10	5/10	8.25/10
Week 3	4/10	4.75/10	7.75/10
Week 4	5/10	5/10	7/10
Week 5	3.75/10	4.25/10	8/10

Week 0 Week 1 Week 2 Week 3 Week 4 Week 5

SECOND VIN

2016 VINTAGE

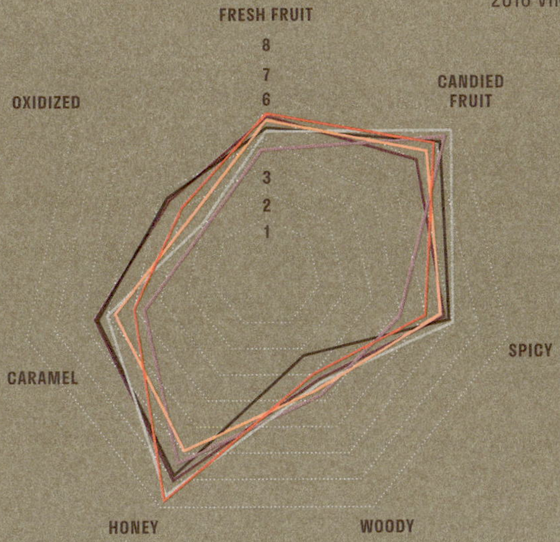

	SPICY	WOODY	HONEY	CARAMEL
Week 0	6/10	3.5/10	7.75/10	5/10
Week 1	5/10	3/10	7.75/10	4/10
Week 2	5.5/10	3.5/10	6/10	4.75/10
Week 3	6/10	2.25/10	7/10	5.5/10
Week 4	4/10	3.75/10	6.5/10	3.75/10
Week 5	5.75/10	3.25/10	7/10	5.5/10

	OXIDIZED	FRESH FRUIT	CANDIED FRUIT
Week 0	2/10	4.5/10	7.75/10
Week 1	3/10	5/10	7/10
Week 2	2.5/10	5/10	6.5/10
Week 3	3.75/10	4.75/10	7/10
Week 4	2/10	3.75/10	7.25/10
Week 5	3.75/10	5/10	6/10

VISITORS' GUIDE

GOLF AND WINE IN THE GIRONDE

The best golf courses in the Gironde and Nouvelle-Aquitaine regions are the **GOLF DU MÉDOC RESORT** in Bordeaux (which offers accommodation and excellent Médoc specialties at its restaurant) and the **GOLF INTERNATIONAL D'ARCACHON**, known in particular for its superb greens.

In Nouvelle-Aquitaine, we recommend the **GOLF DE LA PRÉE**, in La Rochelle, and the beautiful eighteen-hole course at the **GOLF DE ROYAN**, which curves along the site's natural dunes. In the Landes, fans of British-style courses are encouraged to head to **GOLF D'HOSSEGOR**, designed by Arnaud Massy and John Morrison in 1927. Located between the forest and the ocean, the **GOLF DE CHIBERTA** is an all-around favorite, known for its hospitality. Golfers traveling near Limoges must stop off at the **GOLF DE LE PORCELAINE**, where a fairly technical course unfolds in an idyllic setting.

Two agencies can help you prepare the best golf and wine stay:

GOLF EVENTS,
BY MÉLODIE BOURDY
bourdygolf-experiences.com
✉ mb@bourdygolf-experiences.com

GREENS & GRAPES,
BY SYLVIE MCPHILEMY
greensandgrapes.com
✉ lucius@greensandgrapes.com

UNESCO SITES IN THE GIRONDE

The Gironde is home to fourteen UNESCO World Heritage sites (see map on facing page):

THREE MAJOR SITES

1. Bordeaux, Port de la Lune
2. Cordouan lighthouse
3. Eight villages of the jurisdiction of Saint-Émilion (listed in 1999 for their "cultural landscapes")

THREE FORTIFICATIONS OF VAUBAN FORMING THE VERROU OF THE GIRONDE ESTUARY

4. Citadelle de Blaye
5. Fort Pâté
6. Fort Médoc

SITES ON THE WAY OF SAINT JAMES

SOULAC-SUR-MER

7. Notre-Dame-de-la-Fin-des-Terres

BORDEAUX

8. Basilica of Saint Severinus
9. Bordeaux Cathedral (Cathedral of Saint Andrew)
10. Basilica of Saint Michael

LA SAUVE

11. La-Sauve-Majeure Abbey
12. Church of Saint Pierre

BAZAS

13. Cathedral of Saint John the Baptist

ARCHITECTURAL SITE

14. Cité Frugès in Pessac (designed by Le Corbusier)

MÉDOC REGIONAL NATURE PARK

This particularly vast park recently attained the prestigious status of regional nature park. Its varied terrain includes dunes and pine forests at the Pointe de Médoc, where the famous Cordouan lighthouse stands, grazing and cultivated marshes in Nord Médoc, beautiful landscapes along the banks of the estuary, and, of course, vineyards stretching from Margaux to Saint-Christoly, as far as the eye can see.
The park hosts many events, including, in the fall, the opportunity to observe flocks of common cranes arriving to spend the winter, sheltered from predators, in the superb Cousseau Pond nature reserve.
The park also organizes a variety of activities, including visits to sheep farmer Cédric Pérez in Saint-Yzans-de-Médoc. For information and reservations, call +33 (0)5 57 75 18 99 or write to info@pnr-medoc.fr.
In January, there are birdwatching sessions to observe common cranes. Contact the Médoc Atlantique tourism office at +33 (0)5 56 03 21 01 for more information.
pnr-medoc.fr

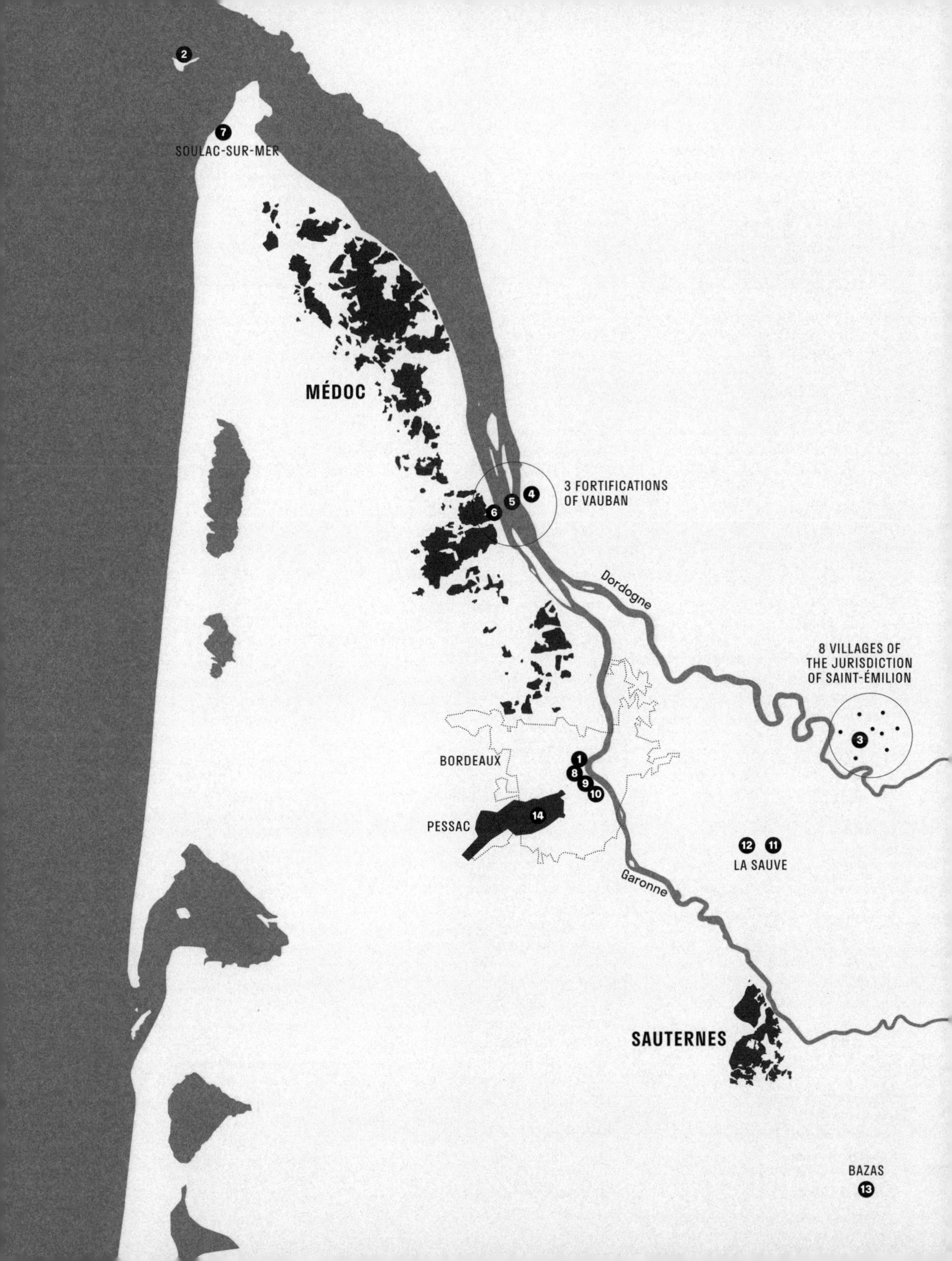
2
7
SOULAC-SUR-MER
MÉDOC
3 FORTIFICATIONS
OF VAUBAN
4
5
6
Dordogne
8 VILLAGES OF
THE JURISDICTION
OF SAINT-ÉMILION
3
BORDEAUX
1
8
9
10
PESSAC
14
12
11
LA SAUVE
Garonne
SAUTERNES
BAZAS
13

TONNELLERIE NADALIÉ

Here, you'll discover one of France's greatest craft traditions. Since 1902, the Nadalié family has been practicing the art of barrel making or "cooperage" in Bordeaux and around the world. Today, the fifth generation maintains this ancestral know-how. The company offers several tours during which you can visit the woodyard stocked with a selection of fine woods, inhale the fragrance of oak in the production workshop, marvel at the alchemy of steam and heat, and admire the natural elegance of master coopers at work. For fun, why not try making a barrel yourself!

A must-visit site for anyone who wants to understand the crucial role wood plays in aging wine

ADDRESS

99 Rue Lafont
33 290 Ludon-Médoc

CONTACT
nadalie.fr

WINE EXCURSIONS

DAY TRIPS

SAUTERNES 1855, GOLDEN WINES

9:15 A.M.
Leave from the Tourist Office in central Bordeaux.

10:15 A.M.
Tour Château de Malle and its Italian gardens.

12 P.M.
Visit a second winemaking estate (tour rotates between Château d'Arche, Château Guiraud, and Château de Myrat), followed by lunch featuring food and wine pairings.

3:30 P.M.
Discover the secrets of making sweet white wines at a third winemaking estate (Château Sigalas-Rabaud, Château Suduirau, or Clos Haut-Peyraguey).

6 P.M. Return to Bordeaux.

PRICE €125 per person
RESERVATIONS bordeaux-tourisme.com

MÉDOC 1855, GRANDS CRUS CLASSÉS D'EXCEPTION

Ten prestigious grands crus classés* take turns welcoming visitors to their estates, where they introduce guests to their terroir and wine, and the history of this exceptional classification.

9:15 A.M.
Leave from the Tourist Office in central Bordeaux. Visit two winemaking estates in the morning (tasting included).

1 P.M.
Lunch at the château.

3:30 P.M.
Visit a winemaking estate (tasting included).

6:30 P.M. Return to Bordeaux.

**Château Batailley, Château Beychevelle, Château Brane-Cantenac, Château Branaire-Ducru, Château de Camensac, Château Haut-Bages Libéral, Château Lagrange, Château Pichon Baron Longueville, Château Prieuré-Lichine, and Château Lascombres*

PRICE €125 per person
RESERVATIONS bordeaux-tourisme.com

GRANDS CRUS: BACK TO THE ROOTS

10 A.M.
Cycle through the Château d'Issan vineyard, followed by a visit and tasting.

12 P.M.
Discover the technical facilities at Château Lafon-Rochet, then eat lunch at the château, followed by a self-guided tour of the vineyard using QR codes.

3 P.M.
Learn about biodiversity, biodynamics, and organic agriculture at Château Pédesclaux.

PRICE €180 per person
RESERVATIONS medoc-tourisme.com

THE LAND OF GRANDS CRUS

Learn about the subtle affinities between wine and chocolate during an unforgettable afternoon at three 1855 grands crus classes, in Pauillac, Saint-Julien, and Margaux.

2:30 P.M.
Meet for a tour of Château Pédesclaux, followed by a tasting of the 2016 vintage of the château's first and second wines paired with two chocolates by Hasnaâ.

4 P.M.
Arrive at Château Léoville Poyferré for a tour of the estate, followed by a tasting of the 2015 and 2005 vintages of the château's *grand vin* and two chocolates by Hasnaâ.

6 P.M.
Aperitif in the garden at Château Marquis de Terme, with a glass of the 2014 vintage of the château's *grand vin* and three original nibbles made with Hasnaâ chocolates.

PRICE €110 per person
RESERVATIONS
✉ lp.visite@leoville-poyferre.fr

WEEKEND GETAWAY

ESCAPE TO SAUTERNES

Less than three hours by train from Paris

- Paris–Langon, Friday evening **5:11 P.M.–7:56 P.M.**
- Langon–Paris, Sunday evening **5:02 P.M.–7:54 P.M.**

FRIDAY EVENING

- Arrive at Château Sigalas Rabaud.
- Check into a guest room and enjoy a welcome glass with a member of the team.
- Dine in the vineyard at La Tour Blanche with sunset views of the Belvédère.

SATURDAY MORNING

- Breakfast at Sigalas Rabaud.
- Take a guided scooter tour around Château d'Yquem, the crown jewel of the 1855 grands crus classés.
- Lunch at the Chapelle at Château Guiraud.

SATURDAY AFTERNOON

- Tree-top tasting at Château de Rayne Vigneau.
- Take the Secrets of Sigalas tour.
- Dine at Château Lafaurie Peyraguey.

SUNDAY

- Breakfast at Sigalas Rabaud.
- Cycle along the Ciron River.
- Chic picnic prepared by the château.
- Return to the train station at **4:45 P.M.**

PRODUCTS FROM NOUVELLE-AQUITAINE

Nouvelle-Aquitaine is home to a wide range of high-quality products and regional specialties, promoted by the Agence de l'Alimentation Nouvelle-Aquitaine (AANA).

MEAT FROM AQUITAINE

LAMB from the Pyrénées, Limousin, Périgord, Poitou-Charentes, and Pauillac
BEEF CATTLE Blonde d'Aquitaine and Blonde Limousine
BAZAS BEEF
PORK from the South West and Limousin
FOIE GRAS DUCK from the South West
FREE-RANGE CHICKEN from Landes, Gascogne, and Périgord

BAZAS FATTED OXEN FESTIVAL

Each year on the Thursday before Mardi Gras, a large traditional celebration is held in the historic city of Bazas. Magnificent fat oxen adorned with ribbons and crowns, and accompanied by stilt walkers, drummers, and fife players, proceed through the city, winding up at the cathedral square, a UNESCO World Heritage Site.

SEAFOOD FROM AQUITAINE

CAVIAR from Aquitaine
OYSTERS from Médoc, Arcachon-Cap Ferret, and Marennes-Oléron

CAVIAR MADE IN FRANCE

The story goes that caviar has been produced on the right bank of the Gironde since 1920 because of a Russian princess. Today, fish farmers in Aquitaine account for more than 70 percent of French caviar production by maintaining centuries-old knowledge and practicing ethical and environmentally conscious farming. The result is every bit as good as anything imported from afar.

ENTRE DEUX CLAIRES

After many years of inactivity, the ancestral practice of oyster farming resumed in 2014 in the northern tip of the Médoc region. The same exceptional terroir that produces the region's wine gives these blue-tinted oysters a slight hazelnut flavor.

FRUIT AND VEGETABLES FROM AQUITAINE

CHERRIES from Itxassou
STRAWBERRIES from Périgord
KIWIS from Adour
MELONS from Haut-Poitou
NUTS AND NUT OIL from Périgord
APPLES from Limousin
PRUNES from Agen
TOMATOES from Marmande
ASPARAGUS from the Sables des Landes and Blayais
PEPPER from Espelette
POTATOES from the Ile de Ré
TRUFFLES from Périgord
CÈPES from Médoc

CHEESE AND DAIRY PRODUCTS FROM AQUITAINE

BUTTER from Charentes Poitou
OSSAU-IRATY CHEESE from Béarn and the Basque country

CABÉCOU CHEESE from Périgord
CHABICHOU CHEESE from Poitou
FEUILLE CHEESE from Limousin
ESTIVE CHEESE
from the Pyrénées Mountains

SPECIALTIES FROM NOUVELLE-AQUITAINE

JAMBON de Bayonne (Bayonne ham)
ANDOUILLE sausage from Béarn
CRÉPINETTE sausage
GRATTON de Lormont (charcuterie)
GRENIER médocain (pork belly charcuterie)
GRILLON Limousin (paté)
ÉCLADE de moules (mussels steamed with pine needles)
GARBURE (meat stew)
PÂTÉ DE POMMES DE TERRE limousin (meat and potato pâté)
BOUDIN aux noix (blood sausage with nuts)
CANELÉ from Bordeaux
GÂTEAU basque
PASTIS landais (traditional brioche usually flavored with rum, vanilla, orange blossom water)
PUITS D'AMOUR from Captieux (choux pastry filled with vanilla cream and caramel)
ROUSQUILLE d'Oloron (shortbread pastry)
TOURTEAU fromager (yogurt-based cake)
TOURTIÈRE landaise (apple tart)
SARMENT du Médoc (vine-shaped chocolates)
NOISETTINES du Médoc (caramelized hazlenuts)
SPRING WATER from the Abatilles spring

JAMBON DE BAYONNE: OFTEN IMITATED, NEVER EQUALED

Back in 1543, Rabelais mentioned **JAMBON DE BAYONNE** (Bayonne ham) in his book *Gargantua*: the meat is a celebrity among the specialties produced in the Bassin de l'Adour, which features on the ham's protected geographical indication. Store it in a dry, cool place, but never in the refrigerator!

THE SURPRISING ORIGIN OF THE CANELÉ

The *canelé*, a small cake flavored with rum and vanilla, appears to date back to the sixteenth century. Its invention is attributed to the Sisters of the Annunciation, who occupied a convent behind the Church of Sainte Eulalie. Legend has it, they would combine wheat salvaged from the port of Bordeaux with leftover egg yolks from the wineries on the Quai des Chartrons (where the whites were used for wine clarification, or "*collage*"). Maritime trade enabled them to procure rum and vanilla to give their little cakes, which were cooked in embers, the unmistakable flavor that we know today.

ABATILLES SPRING WATER

Abatilles spring water is drawn from the deepest spring in France, located near Arcachon. It was discovered in 1923 by a Breton engineer, Louis Le Marié, as he was prospecting. The water travels through 1400 feet (472 m) of limestone, sand, and clay, making it one of the rare French spring waters with a low mineral content. Its unique taste has earned it a place on the tables of many prestigious restaurants.

SPORTS EVENTS

LE MARATHON DES CHÂTEAUX DU MÉDOC (MÉDOC MARATHON)

This festive marathon, packed with wine-themed activities, has taken place every September since 1985. The route follows two loops to the south and north of Pauillac, and winds through about fifty of Bordeaux's châteaux in the Saint-Julien and Saint-Estèphe appellations, and in Médoc and Haut-Médoc. Participants can choose from a variety of packages that include fine dining or walking tours to extend their trip and relive the route at their own pace.
marathondumedoc.com

LA MÉDOCAINE VTT (MÉDOC BICYCLE RALLY)

Participants cycle through the vineyards and the"race" is more like a festive outing. Several thousand cyclists (usually in costume) take off from the starting line in Arsac to ride one of the three suggested routes that run through around fifty châteaux in Margaux, Haut-Medoc, Moulis, and Listrac. The routes are 12½–50 miles (20–80 km) long, and dotted with pit stops, complete with orchestras and wine tastings.

LA RAISIN D'OR

This popular November event takes place in the beautiful vineyards of Sauternes and Barsac, and combines mountain biking, trail running, hiking, and Nordic walking. Participants' efforts are rewarded with views of unforgettable landscapes and a half-bottle of Sauternes to take home.
baroudeursdusauternais.org/accueilraisindor

↑
Route
Médoc Pichon

ADDRESSES

Bordeaux is the French city with the largest number of restaurants per capita. It also boasts the longest pedestrian street in Europe, Rue Sainte-Catherine, with more than two hundred stores stretching three-quarters of a mile (1.2 km).

RESTAURANTS

AU BISTROT
61 Place des Capucins
33 000 Bordeaux
+33 (0)6 63 54 21 14

AU MARQUIS DE TERME
3 Route de Rauzan
33 460 Margaux
+33 (0)5 57 08 25 33
au-marquis-de-terme.com

BIG BISTROT GIRONDIN
64–66 Rue Saint-Rémi
33 000 Bordeaux
+33 (0)5 56 06 10 20

BISTROT BON
5 Rue des Faussets
33 000 Bordeaux
+33 (0)9 74 97 47 82
bistro-bon.fr

CAFÉ LAVINAL
Place du Desquet
33 250 Pauillac
+33 (0)5 57 75 00 09
cafelavinal.com

CENT 33
133 Rue du Jardin-Public
33 000 Bordeaux
+33 (0)5 56 15 90 40
cent33.com

CHEZ DUPONT
45 Rue Notre-Dame
33 000 Bordeaux
+33 (0)5 56 81 49 59
chez-dupont.com

CHEZ MÉMÉ
51 Rue Saint-Rémi
33 000 Bordeaux
+33 (0)5 56 48 03 20
comchezmeme.com

CLAUDE DARROZE ✪
95 Cours du Général Leclerc
33 210 Langon
+33 (0)5 56 63 00 48
darroze.com

COMPTOIR CUISINE
2 Place de la Comédie
33 000 Bordeaux
+33 (0)5 56 56 22 33
comptoircuisine.com

GANACHE
41–43 Rue Saint-Rémi
33 000 Bordeaux
+33 (0)5 57 83 99 02
ganache-Bordeaux.fr

JULIEN CRUÈGE RESTAURANT
245 Rue Turenne
33 000 Bordeaux
+33 (0)5 56 81 97 86
juliencruege.fr

LA BRASSERIE BORDELAISE
50 Rue Saint-Rémi
33 000 Bordeaux
+33 (0)5 57 87 11 91
brasserie-bordelaise.fr

LA CHAPELLE DE GUIRAUD
1 Château-Guiraud
33 210 Sauternes
+33 (0)5 40 24 85 45
lachapelledeguiraud.com

LA MAISON DU FLEUVE
20 Chemin de Seguin
33 360 Camblane et Meynac
+33 (0)5 56 20 06 40
maisonfleuve.com

LA TABLE D'HÔTES–LE QUATRIÈME MUR ✪ BY PHILIPPE ETCHEBEST
Opéra National de Bordeaux
2 Place de la Comédie
33 000 Bordeaux
+33 (0)5 56 02 49 70
quatrieme-mur.com

LA TUPINA
6 Rue Porte-de-la-Monnaie
33 000 Bordeaux
+33 (0)5 56 91 56 37
tupina.com

LA VILLA TOURNY
20 Allée de Tourny
33 000 Bordeaux
+33 (0)5 56 44 60 48

LE 1925
4 Place des Quinconces
33 000 Bordeaux
+33 (0)5 56 52 84 56
le1925.fr

LE BISTROT DU SOMMELIER
163 Rue Georges-Bonnac
33 000 Bordeaux
+33 (0)5 56 96 71 78
bistrotdusommelier.com

LE BONTEMPS
5 Place des Commerces
33 460 Cussac
+33 (0)9 83 02 14 16

LE CHAPON FIN
5 Rue Montesquieu
33 000 Bordeaux
+33 (0)5 56 79 10 10
chapon-fin.com

LE LION D'OR
11 Route de Pauillac
33 460 Arcins
+33 (0)5 56 58 96 79
leliondor-arcins.fr

LE MICHEL'S
15 Rue du Pas-Saint-Georges
33 000 Bordeaux
michelsbistro.fr

LE NOAILLES
12 Allée de Tourny
33 000 Bordeaux
+33 (0)5 56 81 94 45
lenoailles.fr

LE PAVILLON DES BOULEVARDS ✪
12 Rue de la Croix-de-Seguey
33 000 Bordeaux
+33 (0)5 56 81 51 02
lepavillondesboulevards.fr

LE POINT ROUGE
1 Quai de Paludate
33 800 Bordeaux
+33 (0)5 56 94 94 40
lepointrouge-bdx.com

LE PRINCE NOIR ✪
BY VIVIEN DURAND
1 Rue du Prince Noir
33 310 Lormont
+33 (0)5 56 06 12 52
leprincenoir-restaurant.fr

LE SAVOIE
1 Rue de la Trémoille
33 460 Margaux
+33 (0)5 57 88 31 76
lesavoie.net

LE SKIFF CLUB ✪✪
1 Avenue Louis-Gaume
33 115 La Teste-de-Buch
+33 (0)5 56 22 06 06
haaitza.com

L'UNIVERRE
40 Rue Lecocq
33 000 Bordeaux
+33 (0)5 56 23 01 53
univerre-restaurant.com

MAISON NOUVELLE ✪
by Philippe Etchebest
11 Rue Rode
33 000 Bordeaux
+33 (0)5 33 09 46 90
maison-nouvelle.fr

NOMADE
3 Route des Châteaux
33 460 Labarde-Margaux
+33 (0)5 56 35 92 38
restaurant-nomade.fr

PORTE QUINZE
15 Rue Emile-Duployé
33 000 Bordeaux
+33 (0)9 61 65 60 19
restaurantportequinze.fr

TEMPS À NOUVEAU
299 Avenue d'Ares
33 200 Bordeaux
+33 (0)5 56 08 97 35
tempsanouveau.fr

HOTEL-RESTAURANTS

CHÂTEAU LAFAURIE-PEYRAGUEY
HOTEL ✪✪✪✪✪
RESTAURANT LA LALIQUE ✪✪
Lieu-dit Peyraguey
33 210 Sauternes
+33 (0)5 24 22 80 11
lafauriepeyragueylalique.com

HÔTEL DE SÈZE ✪✪✪✪
23 Allées de Tourny
33 000 Bordeaux
+33 (0)5 56 14 16 16
hotel-de-seze.com

HÔTEL LE 23
AUBERGE LES VIGNES
23 Rue Principale
33 210 Sauternes
+33 (0)5 56 76 60 06
aubergelesvignes.fr

INTERCONTINENTAL
GRAND HÔTEL ✪✪✪✪✪
BORDEAUX & PRESSOIR D'ARGENT
GORDON RAMSAY ✪✪
Place de la Comédie
33 000 Bordeaux
+33 (0)5 57 30 44 44
bordeaux.intercontinental.com

LA CO(O)RNICHE ✪✪✪✪✪
46 Avenue Louis-Gaume
33 115 La Teste-de-Buch
+33 (0)5 56 22 72 11
lacoorniche-pyla.com

MAISON D'ESTOURNEL
Route de Poumeys
33 180 Saint-Estèphe
+33 (0)5 56 59 30 25
lamaison-estournel.com

LES TABLES VATEL
114–15 Quai des Chartrons
33 000 Bordeaux
+33 (0)5 56 11 58 88
restaurantvatel.fr

HOTELS

CHÂTEAU CORDEILLAN BAGES ✪✪✪✪
Route des Châteaux
33 250 Pauillac
☎ +33 (0)5 56 59 24 24
cordeillanbages.com

HÔTEL BURDIGALA BORDEAUX ✪✪✪✪
115 Rue Georges-Bonnac
33 000 Bordeaux
☎ +33 (0)5 56 90 16 16
burgigala.com

HÔTEL RENAISSANCE ✪✪✪✪ (MARRIOTT)
16 Rue de Gironde
33 000 Bordeaux
☎ +33 (0)5 19 80 02 00
renaissancebordeauxhotel.com

HÔTEL MOXY ✪✪✪
25 Quai du Maroc
33 000 Bordeaux
☎ +33 (0)5 33 52 13 26
marriott.fr

MAMA SHELTER BORDEAUX
19 Rue Poquelin-Molière
33 000 Bordeaux
☎ +33 (0)5 57 30 45 45
mamashelter.com

RELAIS DU SILENCE RELAIS DU CHÂTEAU D'ARCHE ✪✪✪
Château d'Arche
33 210 Sauternes
☎ +33 (0)5 56 76 67 67
chateau-arche.fr

BED-AND-BREAKFASTS

CHÂTEAU BEYCHEVELLE
33 250 Saint-Julien de Beychevelle
☎ +33 (0)5 56 73 38 10
chateaubeychevelle.com

CHÂTEAU GISCOURS
10 Route de Giscours
33 460 Labarde-Margaux
☎ +33 (0)5 57 97 09 20
giscours.com

CHÂTEAU MAUVESIN BARTON
Route des Ormes
33 480 Moulis en Médoc
☎ +33 (0)5 56 58 41 81
chateau@mauvesin-barton.com

CHÂTEAU ORMES DE PEZ
Route des Ormes
33 180 Saint-Estèphe
☎ +33 (0)5 56 59 30 05
ormesdepez.com

CHÂTEAU DU TERTRE
14 Allée du Tertre
33 460 Arsac
☎ +33 (0)5 57 88 52 52
chateaudutertre.fr

CHÂTEAU LA TOUR CARNET
Darrous
33 112 Saint-Laurent du Médoc
☎ +33 (0)5 57 26 58 65
luxurywineexperience.com

WINE BARS

AUX QUATRE COINS DU VIN
8 Rue de la Devise
33 000 Bordeaux
☎ +33 (0)5 57 34 37 29
aux4coinsduvin.com

CIVB'S BAR À VINS
3 Cours du 30-Juillet
33 000 Bordeaux
☎ +33 (0)5 56 00 43 47
barvin.bordeaux.com

LES TROIS PINARDIERS
2 Rue Georges-Bonnac
33 000 Bordeaux
☎ +33 (0)5 54 52 21 52
les3pinardiers.com

VINS URBAINS
27 Rue des Bahutiers
33 000 Bordeaux
☎ +33 (0)9 52 19 09 37
vinsurbains.fr

WINE MORE TIME
8 Rue Saint-James
33 000 Bordeaux
☎ +33 (0)5 56 52 85 61
winemoretime.fr

↑
Château Cordeillan Bages ✪✪✪✪
Route des Châteaux
33 250 Pauillac
cordeillanbages.com

↑
CIVB's Bar à Vins
3 Cours du 30-Juillet
33 000 Bordeaux
barvin.bordeaux.com

STORES

BACCARAT
5 Cours de l'Intendance
33 000 Bordeaux
+33 (0)5 56 48 37 88
baccarat.fr

BERNARDAUD
5 Cours de l'Intendance
33 000 Bordeaux
+33 (0)5 56 52 02 80
bernardaud.com

CADIOT-BADIE
Chocolatier since 1826
26 Allées de Tourny
33 000 Bordeaux
+33 (0)5 56 44 24 22
cadiot-badie.com

GALERIES LAFAYETTE BORDEAUX
11–19 Rue Sainte-Catherine
33 000 Bordeaux
+33 (0)5 56 90 92 71
galerieslafayette.com

HASNAA
Grands Crus Chocolates
4 Rue de la Vieille-Tour
33 000 Bordeaux
+33 (0)5 56 81 11 40
hasnaa-chocolats.fr

HERMÈS
2 Place Gambetta
33 000 Bordeaux
+33 (0)5 56 52 22 07
hermes.com

L'ALCHIMISTE CAFÉ & BOUTIQUE
12 Rue de la Vieille-Tour
33 000 Bordeaux
+33 (0)9 86 48 37 93
alchimiste-cafes.com

LALIQUE
19 Cours de l'Intendance
33 000 Bordeaux
+33 (0)5 57 34 32 68
lalique.com

LONGCHAMP
18 Rue Voltaire
33 000 Bordeaux
+33 (0)5 56 81 75 58
longchamp.com

LOUIS VUITTON
60 Cours de l'Intendance
33 000 Bordeaux
+33 (0)9 77 40 40 77
louisvuitton.com

MIREMONT TEAROOM
5 Rue Buffon
33 000 Bordeaux
+33 (0)9 83 66 62 88
miremont-bordeaux.com

MOLLAT BOOKSTORE
15 Rue Vital-Carles
33 000 Bordeaux
+33 (0)5 56 56 40 40
mollat.com

CANELÉS

BAILLARDAN
baillardan.com

LA TOQUE CUIVRÉE
la-toque-cuivree.fr

CONSEIL DES GRANDS CRUS CLASSÉS EN 1855

MÉDOC & SAUTERNES

1 Cours du 30 juillet
33000 Bordeaux
+33 (0)5 56 48 47 74
grand-cru-classe-1855.com

CHÂTEAUX: MÉDOC

CHÂTEAU D'ARMAILHAC 51
33 250 Pauillac
+33 (0)5 56 73 20 20
chateau-darmailhac.com

CHÂTEAU BATAILLEY 44
Route de Batailley
33 250 Pauillac
+33 (0)5 56 00 00 70
batailley.com

CHÂTEAU BELGRAVE 55
Darrous
33 112 Saint-Laurent-du-Médoc
+33 (0)5 56 35 53 00
dourthe.com

CHÂTEAU BEYCHEVELLE 40
33 250 Saint-Julien-Beychevelle
+33 (0)5 56 73 20 70
beychevelle.com

CHÂTEAU BOYD-CANTENAC 25
11 Route de Jean Faure
33 460 Margaux-Cantenac
+33 (0)5 57 88 90 82
boyd-cantenac.fr

CHÂTEAU BRANAIRE-DUCRU 35
1 Chemin du Bourdieu
33 250 Saint-Julien-Beychevelle
+33 (0)5 56 59 25 86
branaire.com

CHÂTEAU BRANE-CANTENAC 13
Chemin de Benqueyre
33 460 Margaux-Cantenac
+33 (0)5 57 88 83 33
brane-cantenac.com

CHÂTEAU CALON SÉGUR 30
33 180 Saint-Estèphe
+33 (0)5 56 59 30 08
calon-segur.fr

CHÂTEAU DE CAMENSAC 56
Route de Saint-Julien
33 112 Saint-Laurent-du-Médoc
+33 (0)5 56 59 41 69
chateaucamensac.com

CHÂTEAU CANTEMERLE 60
33 460 Macau
+33 (0)5 57 97 02 82
cantemerle.com

CHÂTEAU CANTENAC BROWN 26
Route d'Arsac
33 460 Margaux
+33 (0)5 57 88 81 81
cantenacbrown.com

CHÂTEAU CLERC MILON 58
Lieu-dit Mousset
33 250 Pauillac
+33 (0)5 56 73 20 20
chateau-clerc-milon.com

CHÂTEAU COS D'ESTOURNEL 17
33 180 Saint-Estèphe
+33 (0)5 56 73 15 50
estournel.com

CHÂTEAU COS LABORY 57
33 180 Saint-Estèphe
+33 (0)5 56 59 30 22
cos-labory.com

CHÂTEAU CROIZET-BAGES 59
9 Rue du Port-de-la-Verrerie
33 250 Pauillac
+33 (0)5 56 59 01 62
domaines-quie.com

CHÂTEAU DAUZAC 50
1 Avenue Georges Johnston
33 460 Labarde
+33 (0)5 57 88 98 51
chateaudauzac.com

CHÂTEAU DESMIRAIL 29
28 Avenue de la 5e République
33 460 Margaux-Cantenac
+33 (0)5 57 88 34 33
desmirail.com

CHÂTEAU DUCRU-BEAUCAILLOU 16
33 250 Saint-Julien-Beychevelle
+33 (0)5 56 73 16 73
chateau-ducru-beaucaillou.com

CHÂTEAU DUHART-MILON 36
Rue Étienne Dieuzede
33 250 Pauillac
+33 (0)5 56 59 03 60
lafite.com

CHÂTEAU DURFORT-VIVENS 10
3 Rue du Général de Gaulle
33 460 Margaux-Cantenac
+33 (0)5.57.88.31.02
durfort-vivens.fr

CHÂTEAU FERRIÈRE 31
33 bis Rue de La Trémoille
33 460 Margaux-Cantenac
+33 (0)5 57 88 76 65
ferriere.com

CHÂTEAU GISCOURS 23
10 Route de Giscours
33 460 Labarde
+33 (0)5 57 97 09 09
giscours.fr

CHÂTEAU GRAND-PUY DUCASSE 47
4 Quai Antoine Ferchaud
33 250 Pauillac
+33 (0)5 56 59 00 40
grandpuyducasse.fr

CHÂTEAU GRAND-PUY-LACOSTE 46
33 250 Pauillac
+33 (0)5 56 59 06 66
grand-puy-lacoste.com

CHÂTEAU GRUAUD LAROSE 11
33 250 Saint-Julien Beychevelle
+33 (0)5 56 73 15 20
gruaud-larose.com

CHÂTEAU HAUT-BAGES LIBÉRAL 53
18 Balogues
33 250 Pauillac
+33 (0)5 56 59 11 88
hautbagesliberal.com

CHÂTEAU HAUT-BATAILLEY 45
667 Petit-Batailley
33 250 Pauillac
+33 (0)5 56 73 24 00
chateau-haut-batailley.com

CHÂTEAU HAUT-BRION 5
135 Avenue Jean Jaurès
33 608 Pessac
+33 (0)5 56 00 29 30
haut-brion.com

CHÂTEAU D'ISSAN 20
Chemin de la Ménagerie
33 460 Cantenac
+33 (0)5 57 88 35 91
chateau-issan.com

CHÂTEAU KIRWAN 19
Chemin de Kirwan
33 460 Margaux-Cantenac
+33 (0)5 57 88 71 00
chateau-kirwan.com

CHÂTEAU LAFITE ROTHSCHILD 1
33 250 Pauillac
+33 (0)5 56 73 18 18
lafite.com

CHÂTEAU LAFON-ROCHET 39
Blanquet ouest
33 180 Saint-Estèphe
+33 (0)5 56 59 32 06
lafon-rochet.com

CHÂTEAU LAGRANGE 21
33 250 Saint-Julien-Beychevelle
+33 (0)5 56 73 38 38
chateau-lagrange.com

CHÂTEAU LA LAGUNE 28
81 Avenue de l'Europe
33 290 Ludon-Médoc
+33 (0)5 57 88 82 77
chateau-lalagune.com

CHÂTEAU LANGOA-BARTON 22
33 250 Saint-Julien-Beychevelle
+33 (0)5 56 59 06 05
langoa-barton.com

CHÂTEAU LASCOMBES 12
1 Cours de Verdun
33 460 Margaux-Cantenac
+33 (0)5 57 88 70 66
chateau-lascombes.com

CHÂTEAU LATOUR 2
Saint-Lambert
33 250 Pauillac
+33 (0)5 56 73 19 80
chateau-latour.com

CHÂTEAU LÉOVILLE BARTON 9
33 250 Saint-Julien-Beychevelle
+33 (0)5 56 59 06 05
leoville-barton.com

CHÂTEAU LÉOVILLE POYFERRÉ 8
38 Rue de Saint-Julien
33 250 Saint-Julien-Beychevelle
+33 (0)5 56 59 08 30
leoville-poyferre.fr

CHÂTEAU LYNCH-BAGES 48
33 250 Pauillac
+33 (0)5 56 73 19 31
lynchbages.com

CHÂTEAU LYNCH-MOUSSAS 49
33 250 Pauillac
+33 (0)5 56 00 00 70
lynch-moussas.com

CHÂTEAU MALESCOT SAINT-EXUPÉRY 24
16 Rue Georges Mandel
33 460 Margaux-Cantenac
+33 (0)5 57 88 97 20
malescot.com

CHÂTEAU MARGAUX 3
33 460 Margaux-Cantenac
+33 (0)5 57 88 83 83
chateau-margaux.com

CHÂTEAU MARQUIS D'ALESME 32
7 Rue de la Trémoille
33 460 Margaux-Cantenac
+33 (0)5 57 81 13 20
marquisdalesme.wine

CHÂTEAU MARQUIS DE TERME 42
3 Route de Rauzan
33 460 Margaux
+33 (0)5 57 88 30 01
chateau-marquis-de-terme.com

CHÂTEAU MONTROSE 18
3 Grand Vignolles
33 180 Saint-Estèphe
+33 (0)5 56 59 30 12
chateau-montrose.com

CHÂTEAU MOUTON ROTHSCHILD 4
33 250 Pauillac
+33 (0)5 56 73 20 20
chateau-mouton-rothschild.com

CHÂTEAU PALMER 27
33 460 Margaux-Cantenac
+33 (0)5 57 88 72 72
chateau-palmer.com

CHÂTEAU PÉDESCLAUX 54
Route de Pédesclaux
33 250 Pauillac
+33 (0)5 57 73 64 64
chateau-pedesclaux.com

CHÂTEAU PICHON BARON 14
33 250 Pauillac
+33 (0)5 56 73 17 17
pichonbaron.com

CHÂTEAU PICHON LONGUEVILLE COMTESSE DE LALANDE 15
Comtesse de Lalande
33 250 Pauillac
+33 (0)5 56 73 17 17
pichon-lalande.com

CHÂTEAU PONTET-CANET 43
33 250 Pauillac
+33 (0)5 56 59 04 04
pontet-canet.com

CHÂTEAU POUGET 37
11 Rue de Jean Fauré
33 460 Margaux-Cantenac
+33 (0)5 57 88 90 82
chateau-pouget.com

CHÂTEAU PRIEURÉ-LICHINE 41
34 Avenue de la 5e République
33 460 Cantenac
+33 (0)5 57 88 36 28
prieure-lichine.fr

CHÂTEAU RAUZAN-GASSIES 7
1 Rue Alexis Millardet
33 460 Margaux
+33 (0)5 57 88 71 88
domaines-quie.com

CHÂTEAU RAUZAN-SÉGLA 6
Rue Alexis Millardet
33 460 Margaux
+33 (0)5 57 88 82 10
chateaurauzansegla.com

CHÂTEAU SAINT-PIERRE 33
33 250 Saint-Julien-Beychevelle
+33 (0)5 56 59 08 18
domaines-henri-martin.com

CHÂTEAU TALBOT 34
33 250 Saint-Julien-Beychevelle
+33 (0)5 56 73 21 50
chateau-talbot.com

CHÂTEAU DU TERTRE 52
14 Allée du Tertre
33 460 Arsac
+33 (0)5 57 88 52 52
chateaudutertre.fr

CHÂTEAU LA TOUR CARNET 38
Darrous
33 112 Saint-Laurent-Médoc
+33 (0)5 57 26 38 34
bernard-magrez.com

CHÂTEAUX: SAUTERNES & BARSAC

CHÂTEAU D'ARCHE 77
33 210 Sauternes
+33 (0)5 56 76 67 67
chateau-arche.fr

CHÂTEAU BROUSTET 79
1 Broustet
33 720 Barsac
+33 (0)5 47 74 78 00
vignoblesdeterroirs.com

CHÂTEAU CAILLOU 81
9 Caillou
33 720 Barsac
+33 (0)5 56 27 16 38
chateaucaillou.com

CHÂTEAU CLIMENS 68
33 720 Barsac
+33 (0)5 56 27 15 33
chateau-climens.fr

CLOS HAUT-PEYRAGUEY 64
1 Peyraguey
33 210 Bommes
+33 (0)5 57 26 38 38
bernard-magrez.com

CHÂTEAU COUTET 67
33 720 Barsac
+33 (0)5 56 27 15 46
chateaucoutet.com

CHÂTEAU DOISY DAËNE 74
15 Gravas
33 720 Barsac
+33 (0)5 56 62 96 51
denisdubourdieu.com

CHÂTEAU DOISY-DUBROCA 75
33 720 Barsac
+33 (0)5 56 62 96 51
denisdubourdieu.com

CHÂTEAU DOISY-VÉDRINES 76
33 720 Barsac
+33 (0)5 56 27 15 13

CHÂTEAU FILHOT 78
Route de Filhot
33 210 Sauternes
+33 (0)5 56 76 61 09
filhot.fr

CHÂTEAU GUIRAUD 69
1 Château Guiraud
33 210 Sauternes
+33 (0)5.56.76.61.01
chateauguiraud.com

CHÂTEAU LAFAURIE-PEYRAGUEY 63
33 210 Bommes
+33 (0)5 56 76 60 54
chateau-
lafaurie-peyraguey.com

CHÂTEAU LAMOTHE DESPUJOLS 86
19 Rue Principale
33 210 Sauternes
+33 (0)5 56 76 67 89
lamothe-despujols.com

CHÂTEAU LAMOTHE GUIGNARD 87
2 Lamothe Ouest
33 210 Sauternes
+33 (0)5 56 76 60 28
chateau-lamothe-guignard.fr

CHÂTEAU LA TOUR BLANCHE 62
33 210 Bommes
+33 (0)5 57 98 02 73
tour-blanche.com

CHÂTEAU DE MALLE 83
33 210 Preignac
+33 (0)5 56 62 36 86
chateaudemalle.fr

CHÂTEAU DE MYRAT 73
33 720 Barsac
+33 (0)5 56 27 09 06
chateaudemyrat.fr

CHÂTEAU NAIRAC 80
81 Avenue Aristide Briand
33 720 Barsac
+33 (0)5 56 27 16 16
chateaunairac.com

CHÂTEAU RABAUD-PROMIS 71
33 210 Bommes
+33 (0)5 56 76 67 38
rabaud-promis.com

CHÂTEAU DE RAYNE VIGNEAU 65
4 Le Vigneau
33 210 Bommes
+33 (0)5 56 76 64 05
raynevigneau.fr

CHÂTEAU RIEUSSEC 70
33 210 Fargues
+33 (0)5 57 98 14 14
lafite.com

CHÂTEAU ROMER 85
33 210 Preignac
+33 (0)5 57 55 55 44
janoueixfrancois.com

CHÂTEAU ROMER DU HAYOT 84
33 210 Sauternes
+33 (0)5 56 27 15 37
vignobles-du-hayot.com

CHÂTEAU SIGALAS RABAUD 72
1 Sigalas-Rabaud
33 210 Bommes
+33 (0)5 57 31 07 45
chateau-sigalas-rabaud.com

CHÂTEAU SUAU 82
33 210 Sauternes
+33 (0)5 56 64 16 16
chateausuau.com

CHÂTEAU SUDUIRAUT 66
33 210 Preignac
+33 (0)5 56 63 61 92
suduiraut.com

CHÂTEAU D'YQUEM 61
33 210 Sauternes
+33 (0)5 57 98 07 07
yquem.fr

ACKNOWLEDGMENTS

This book was conceived as a guide to the wine tourism activities on offer from the châteaux included in the 1855 Classification of Bordeaux Wines and to show that their doors are open to the world.

This guide is the result of the close collaboration and commitment of a group of individuals who are passionate about their profession: Lise Latrille, Anne Cuvelier, Aymone Fabre, Clémence Planty, Laure de Lambert-Compeyrot, Mélissa Avril, Sandrine Chamfrault, Maïsa Mendonca, Charles Thuillier, Vincent Labergère, Marc Verpaalen, and Sylvain Boivert.

The Conseil des Grands Crus Classés du Médoc en 1855 would like to extend its sincere thanks to Flammarion, and in particular to Ronite Tubiana for her professionalism and her passion for creating beautiful illustrated books; to Kate Mascaro for her experience and enthusiasm; to Ryma Bouzid, for her efficiency and kindness; and to Eric Chenebier, for his attentiveness and his depth of understanding of our region.

We would also like to thank all those who contributed to this book: Stéphane Bern, a great defender of French patrimony, who honored us with his support; our friend and incredible sommelier Eric Beaumard; the wonderful professor Fabrizio Bucella, for his shrewd analyses and experiments; history professor Stéphanie Lavaud, for his encyclopedic knowledge of Sauternes; and the most French of Americans, Karen Taylor, a longtime champion of France in the United States. Special thanks to Charlotte Lagrange for her diligent contribution to this guide.

Finally, the Conseil des Grands Crus Classés 1855 would like to pay homage to Ghislaine Bavoillot, editor and director of collections at Flammarion for many years. Her quest for perfection was never-ending. Thanks to her, in 2005 the Grands Crus Classés 1855 celebrated the classification's 150th anniversary in the most remarkable way: with a unique and magnificent illustrated book. Ghislaine Bavoillot introduced us to Franck Ferrand, an exceptional author, and enabled us to reach the entire world in many languages (eight in all: French, English, German, Dutch, Italian, Czech, Japanese, and Chinese), with nearly one hundred thousand copies sold and thousands of related press articles. *Merci Gisou.*

FRENCH EDITION
Art de Vivre Department
Editorial Director
Ronite Tubiana
Editorial Manager
Ryma Bouzid-Fuchs
Text
Eric Chenebier
Design and Typesetting
Atelier Marge Design

ENGLISH EDITION
Editorial Director
Kate Mascaro
Editor
Helen Adedotun
Translation from the French
Kate Robinson
Copyediting
Lindsay Porter

Production
Louisa Hanifi and Julie Hautecourt
Color Separation
Atelier Frédéric Claudel, Paris
Printed in Slovenia
by Florjancic Tisk

Simultaneously published in French as *Route 1855: Bordeaux Châteaux, Médoc & Sauternes*

87, quai Panhard et Levassor
75647 Paris Cedex 13

editions.flammarion.com

22 23 24 3 2 1
ISBN: 978-2-08-028092-3
Legal Deposit: 06/2022

UNWTO
AFFILIATE MEMBER

PHOTOGRAPHIC CREDITS
©
C. Goussart
G. Vincent
G. Uféras
XTU Architects
L. Gauthier
E. Bouloumié
S. Le Clech
C. Formé-Bècherat
B. Braastad
N. Young — Foster + Partners
Saison d'Or Mathieu Anglada
I. Mathie
Vinexia
C. Durand-Moldawan
M. Cont — Les Editions d'Autils
Taylor & Yandell
É. Vene
R. Smuin
S. Billant
Ch. Jouniaux
Ch. Goussard
L. Walter
N. Seurot
R. Escher
A. Benoît
A-E. Thion
Anaka
N. Duffaure
B. Bolton
G. Gardette
M. Garçon
F. Poincet
V. Bengold
F. Nivelle
Deepix
G. Uféras
S. Chapuis
N. Coster
Studio Tonelli
C. Planty
M. Anglada
M. Boudot
M. Palace
F. Encuentra — BarbotStudio